# ALICE IN PUZZLE-LAND

*A Carrollian Tale for Children Under Eighty*

## RAYMOND M. SMULLYAN

With an introduction by Martin Gardner

ILLUSTRATED BY GREER FITTING

*William Morrow and Company, Inc. / New York   1982*

OTHER BOOKS BY RAYMOND SMULLYAN

*Theory of Formal Systems*
*First-Order Logic*
*The Tao Is Silent*
*What Is the Name of This Book?*
*This Book Needs No Title*
*The Chess Mysteries of Sherlock Holmes*
*The Chess Mysteries of the Arabian Knights*
*The Lady or the Tiger?*

**Library of Congress Cataloging in Publication Data**

Smullyan, Raymond M.
  Alice in puzzle-land.

  1. Puzzles.   I. Carroll, Lewis, 1832–1898.
Alice's adventures in wonderland.   II. Title.
GV1493.S624      793.73      82-2215
ISBN 0-688-00748-1          AACR2

Printed in the United States of America
FIRST EDITION

1 2 3 4 5 6 7 8 9 10

BOOK DESIGN BY HELENE BERINSKY

# Preface

This book, like *Alice's Adventures in Wonderland* and *Through the Looking-Glass*, is truly for readers of all ages. By this I do not mean that all of it is for every age, but for every age, some of it is for that age. For example, the extremely elementary puzzles of Chapter Four are particularly for the very young reader who has not yet learned algebra (and, as the Gryphon wisely says, "You don't needs no algebra!"). At the opposite extreme are the prize puzzles of Chapters Five and Nine; these will intrigue the expert as much as the beginner. Chapter Ten has a special and unusual status.

This year (1982) marks the one-hundred-fiftieth anniversary of the birth of Lewis Carroll, to whom this book is dedicated. I believe Carroll would have particularly enjoyed the Humpty chapter, which deals with paradoxes (one of Carroll's favorite themes), but in the inimitable manner of Humpty Dumpty. This chapter was great fun to write (as were all the other chapters!). Indeed, the whole project of re-creating the spirit of Carroll's writings has been a delight from beginning to end.

My heartfelt thanks go to Greer Fitting, for all the lovely illustrations; to Maria Guarnaschelli, for her excellent editorship; and to Iver Kern, who carefully went through the entire manuscript and provided a host of helpful suggestions.

—RAYMOND M. SMULLYAN

*Elka Park, New York*
*January 1, 1982*

# Contents

# Introduction

Raymond Smullyan is a unique set of personalities that includes a philosopher, logician, mathematician, musician, magician, humorist, writer, and maker of marvelous puzzles. Because he is a skillful writer and humorist, he enjoys presenting his puzzles in narrative forms that often parody great works of popular fiction. And he does this so well that his puzzle books are, incredibly, a pleasure to read even if you never try to solve a single puzzle!

Ray's first puzzle book (I call him Ray because we are old friends) was titled *What Is the Name of This Book?* It introduced his knights (who speak only truth), his knaves (who always lie), and such characters as Inspector Craig, Bellini and Cellini, Count Dracula, and Lewis Carroll's Alice and the creatures of Wonderland. Of course readers who actually worked on the puzzles of this book, whatever its name, found the book doubly rewarding, and at the end they were given a remarkable bonus—an insight into Kurt Gödel's famous proof, the greatest of modern mathematical discoveries.

Ray's first collection of original chess problems, *The Chess Mysteries of Sherlock Holmes*, surrounds each problem with a pastiche about Holmes and Watson. So faithful are these tales to the spirit of the canon that Sherlockians who never play a game of chess can enjoy them for the dialogue alone. A second collection of chess problems, *The Chess Mysteries of the Arabian Knights*, embed the problems in parodies of the tales of Scheherazade.

In the volume you now hold, Alice and her friends are back again for a puzzle romp behind the Looking-Glass that will please Carrollians as much as the first book of chess puzzles pleased Baker Street Irregulars. Ray has done it again. His characters not only talk and behave exactly like the originals, but the book also swarms with typically Carrollian word play, logic and metalogic problems, and dark philosophical paradoxes. In Carroll's nonsense world there were two Alices: the imaginary one and his real-life child-friend Alice Liddell. In Ray's nonsense world there are also two Alices: a friend of Ray's, and the imaginary Alice of his first book. Carroll would have loved them both. And he would have been delighted by Ray's looking-glass package that unwraps itself only when you try to wrap it, and a hundred other whimsies that Carroll might have thought of himself if he had been capable of dreaming up Raymond Smullyan.

As always in Ray's books, curious metaphysical questions have a way of catching you by surprise. For example, when Humpty Dumpty tells Alice she should think of everything, Alice sensibly declares this to be impossible.

"I never said you *could*," Humpty replies. "I merely said you *should*."

"But is it reasonable to say that I should do something that I cannot do?"

"That is an interesting problem in Moral Philosophy," answers Humpty, "but that would take us too far afield."

It would indeed! Ray does not tell you, but Humpty has raised a famous problem known as Hintikka's paradox, after Jaako Hintikka, a leader of a fashionable new school of "possible worlds" philosophers. Is it proper to call morally wrong something a person cannot do? Hintikka has a notorious argument designed to show it is wrong to try to do something impossible. There is now a large literature on this strange question, which belongs to a type of modal logic called deontic logic. We learned from Carroll that Humpty is an expert on classical logic and semantics. Now we learn from Ray that the egg is also an expert on modal logic!

A page or two later, Humpty bewilders Alice with an amazing one-sentence version of another famous paradox that goes under such names as the "unexpected examination" and the "unexpected hanging." (You can read about it in the first chapter of my book, *The Unexpected Hanging*.) Humpty is not sure whether his elegant compression of this puzzle is a genuine paradox or not, and you won't be either after you understand it. As Humpty exclaims, "That's the beautiful part of it!"

In his chapter about the White Knight, Carroll tells us: "Of all the strange things that Alice saw in her journey Through the Looking-Glass, this was the one that she always remembered most clearly. Years afterwards she could bring the whole scene back again, as if it had been only yesterday. . . ."

Ray has not forgotten. "Of all Alice's puzzle-adventures in the Looking-Glass," he begins Chapter Nine, "the ones that follow were those she remembered most vividly. For years after, she kept telling her friends these fascinating and unusual puzzles." Yes, and you would swear it is Carroll's own White Knight who has tumbled off his horse into Ray's pages.

At the close of Carroll's second Alice book, Alice wonders if she has dreamed about the Red King, or if she is only a sort of thing in the Red King's dream. In his last two chapters, Ray weaves brilliant puzzle themes around the act of dreaming. His book ends with the Red King presenting Alice with a question about dreams that is so confusing and so deep that, as Carroll did, Ray wisely leaves it unanswered.

No one can read this book, or any of Ray's books, without becoming more aware of the mystery of being, of the difficulty of distinguishing what is true from what is false, or what is real from what is unreal. That's the beautiful part of them. And you close this book knowing that Ray has shown you only a small part of the fantastic puzzle tricks he has up his conjuror's sleeves, that he is speaking through the Duchess when she says, "As to *confusing* puzzles, these are nothing compared to some I *could* tell you if I chose!"

—MARTIN GARDNER

*Hendersonville, North Carolina*

🜲 *Part I*

# WONDERLAND PUZZLES

## CHAPTER 1

# *Which Alice?*

It all started at Alice's birthday party. Not the Alice in Wonderland, but my friend Alice. How the other Alice entered the story will soon be apparent. Of course Alice's younger brother, Tony, was there, as well as her friends Michael, Lillian, and several others.

After many games and magic tricks, the whole company wanted to hear some logic puzzles.

"Here's a nice one," I said. "There are two identical twins. One of them always lies and the other one always tells the truth."

"What are their names?" asked Tony.

"One of them is named *John*," I replied.

"Such a common name!" exclaimed Michael. "It seems that just about every Tom, Dick and Harry is called *John*!"

I could not help being somewhat puzzled by this remark.

"What is the name of the other brother?" asked Tony.

"I don't remember," I replied.

"Why don't you remember?" asked Michael.

"I have no idea *why* I don't remember," I answered, "and the name of the other brother doesn't matter."

"Is John the one who lies, or is it his brother?" asked Lillian.

"Good question," I answered, "but unfortunately no one knows whether it is John or his brother who lies."

"Then what is the problem?" asked Alice.

"The problem is this: Suppose you meet the two brothers and you wish to find out which one is John. You may ask only one question to one of them, and the question must be answerable by *yes* or *no*. Furthermore, the question may not exceed three words. What would you ask?"

"Three words!" cried Michael in astonishment.

"Yes, three words," I replied. "Actually," I continued, "this makes the problem easier; there are not that many three-word questions!"

"I have it!" said one of Alice's friends. "Ask one of them, 'Are you John?'"

"That won't work," said Michael. "Suppose he answers yes. What would that prove? Nothing at all; he might be lying or telling the truth."

"I have it!" said another. "Ask one of them, 'Is water wet?'"

The group thought about this for a moment.

"That won't work," said Alice. "If he answers yes, you'll know that he tells the truth, and if he answers no, you'll know that he is the one who lies, but you still won't know whether or not he is John."

"Exactly!" I replied.

"But you'll know whether or not he lies," said Tony.

"True," I replied, "but that's not the problem. The problem is not to find the liar, but to find out which one is John."

"I have an idea!" said another. "How about asking the question 'Do you lie?'"

"That's a useless question!" said Lillian. "You should know in advance that the answer you will get will be no—regardless of whether you addressed the liar or the truth-teller."

"Why is that?" asked another.

"Because," replied Lillian, "a truth-teller would never lie and claim to be a liar, and a liar would never truthfully admit he is a liar. So in either case you will get no for an answer."

"Very good," I said.

"Then what question will work?" asked Tony.

"Ah, that's the puzzle you are to solve!"

Well, the group bandied the problem about for a while, and finally came up with a three-word question which does work. Can you find such a question? (The solution is given in the back of the book.)

\*   \*   \*

After they solved the problem, Alice asked, "Suppose that instead of trying to find out which one is John, you wanted to find out whether John is the liar or the one who tells the truth. Could this be done with only one question?"

"Oh, certainly!" I replied.

"But not with a three-word question," suggested Tony.

I thought about this for a moment.

"As a matter of fact there *is* a three-word question that will do this," I finally responded.

Can the reader find a three-word question that will determine not which one is John, but whether John lies?

After the refreshments were served, the company all wanted some more logic puzzles.

"In one of your books," said Alice, "you had some puzzles about Alice in the Looking-Glass. Can you tell us some more?"

"I wrote about *you* in the Looking-Glass?" I asked.

"No, not *me!*" said Alice excitedly. "The other Alice!"

"Which Alice was that?" I asked.

"The one in the Looking-Glass!"

"Oh, in other words your reflection!"

"No, no, no!" shouted Alice. "Not *my* reflection. It had nothing at all to do with *me*. It was the Alice of Lewis Carroll's story!"

"Oh!" I answered innocently.

"Well, will you tell us some more of those stories?"

I thought for a moment. "How about some stories about Alice in Wonderland?" I asked.

"I was never *in* Wonderland," Alice replied.

"No! No! No!" I shouted excitedly. "I didn't mean *you*—I meant the other Alice!"

"Which Alice?" asked Alice.

"Why, the one in the story!" I answered, still excited. (At this point all the company laughed with delight that Alice had just succeeded in playing the same trick on me that I had played on her!)

"I was only kidding," said Alice, laughing, "just like you were. Anyway, I'd love to hear some of your stories about Alice in Wonderland."

This got us started.

## CHAPTER 2

# *Who Stole the Tarts?*

The Queen of Hearts, she made some tarts
  All on a summer's day;
The Knave of Hearts, he stole the tarts
  And took them quite away!
           —OLD NURSERY RHYME

⚜1

THE FIRST TALE "How about making us some nice tarts?" the King of Hearts asked the Queen of Hearts one cool summer day.

"What's the sense of making tarts without jam?" said the Queen furiously. "The jam is the best part!"

"Then use jam," said the King.

"I can't!" shouted the Queen. "My jam has been stolen!"

"Really!" said the King. "This is quite serious! Who stole it?"

"How do you expect *me* to know who stole it? If I knew, I would have had it back long ago and the miscreant's head in the bargain!"

Well, the King had his soldiers scout around for the missing jam, and it was found in the house of the March Hare, the Mad Hatter, and the Dormouse. All three were promptly arrested and tried.

"Now, now!" exclaimed the King at the trial. "I want to get to the bottom of this! I don't like people coming into my kitchen and stealing my jam!"

"Why not?" asked one of the guinea pigs.

"Suppress that guinea pig!" shouted the Queen. The guinea pig

7

was promptly suppressed. (Those who have read *Alice's Adventures in Wonderland* will recall the meaning of the word *suppress:* The officers of the court put the guinea pig into a canvas bag, which tied up at the mouth with strings, and sat upon it.)

"Now then," said the King, after the commotion of suppressing the guinea pig had died down, "I want to get to the bottom of this!"

"You've already said that," remarked a second guinea pig. (This guinea pig was also promptly suppressed.)

"Did *you* by any chance steal the jam?" the King asked the March Hare.

"I never stole the jam!" pleaded the March Hare. (At this point all the remaining guinea pigs cheered, and were all promptly suppressed.)

"What about *you?*" the King roared to the Hatter, who was trembling like a leaf. "Are you by any chance the culprit?"

The Hatter was unable to utter a word; he just stood there gasping and sipping his tea.

"If he has nothing to say, that only proves his guilt," said the Queen, "so off with his head immediately!"

"No, no!" pleaded the Hatter. "One of us stole it, but it wasn't me!"

"Make a note of that!" said the King to the jury. "This evidence might turn out to be quite important!"

"And what about *you?*" continued the King to the Dormouse. "What do you have to say about all this? Did the March Hare and the Hatter both tell the truth?"

"At least one of them did," replied the Dormouse, who then fell asleep for the rest of the trial.

As subsequent investigation revealed, the March Hare and the Dormouse were not both speaking the truth.

Who stole the jam? (Solution on page 140.)

♛ 2

THE SECOND TALE "Now we have the jam back," said the King, "so you can make us some tarts."

"How can I make tarts without flour?" asked the Queen.

"You mean the flour was stolen?" cried the King.

"Yes!" said the Queen. "Find the miscreant, and take his head off!"

"Now, now," said the King, "let's not be hasty!"

Still, the flour had to be found. Sure enough, it was found in the home of the March Hare, the Mad Hatter, and the Dormouse, so these three were promptly arrested and tried.

At the trial, the March Hare claimed that the Hatter stole it. The Hatter and the Dormouse also made statements, but for some reason the statements were not recorded, so I cannot tell you what they were. Anyhow, as it turned out, only one of the three had stolen the flour, and he was the only one of the three who told the truth.

Who stole the flour?

👑 3

THE THIRD TALE "Well, here is your flour," said the King happily, "so now you can make the tarts."

"Make tarts without pepper?" asked the Queen.

"Pepper!" said the King incredulously. "You mean you use pepper in your tarts?"

"Not much," replied the Queen.

"And I suppose it was stolen!"

"Of course!" said the Queen. "Find the pepper, and when you have found out who stole it, then off with his—"

"Now, now!" said the King.

Well, the pepper had to be found, of course. Now, as you all know, people who steal pepper never tell the truth.

"What!" said Alice (not the Alice in Wonderland, but the Alice of this party). "I never heard that before!"

"You haven't?" I said in mock surprise.

"Of course not! What's more, I don't believe anybody else has either! Have any of you heard that before?"

The children all shook their heads negatively.

"Well," I said, "for purposes of this story, let's assume that people who steal pepper never tell the truth."

"All right," said Alice, a bit hesitantly.

So, to continue the story, the most obvious suspect was the Duchess's cook. At the trial she made but one statement: "I know who stole the pepper!"

Assuming that people who steal pepper always lie, is the cook guilty or innocent?


### 4

SO, WHO STOLE THE PEPPER? Well, the King's next suspects were the March Hare, the Mad Hatter, and the Dormouse. Soldiers were sent to their house, but no pepper was found. Still, they might be hiding it somewhere, so they were arrested on general principles.

At the trial the March Hare claimed that the Hatter was innocent and the Hatter claimed that the Dormouse was innocent. The Dormouse mumbled some statement in his sleep, but it was not recorded.

As it turned out, no innocent one made a false statement and (we recall) people who steal pepper never make true statements. Also, the pepper was stolen by only one creature. Which, if any of the three, is guilty?

♛5

THEN WHO DID STEAL THE PEPPER? "My, my, this is really a difficult case!" said the King.

The next suspects, curiously enough, were the Gryphon, the Mock Turtle, and the Lobster. At the trial, the Gryphon said that the Mock Turtle was innocent and the Mock Turtle said that the Lobster was guilty.

Again, no innocent one lied and no guilty one told the truth.

Who stole the pepper?

♛6

A METAPUZZLE  Alice (my friend) interrupted my story at this point and said:

"You know, Raymond, your choice of characters for the last puzzle was not wholly satisfactory."

I thought for a few moments, and suddenly realized what a remarkably clever girl Alice is!

Those of you who have read *Alice in Wonderland,* can you see why?

♛7

THE FOURTH TALE  "That certainly cost me a lot of work finding the pepper," said the King angrily, "and I doubt that the tarts will be all that much the better for it! Pepper indeed!" continued the King. "Why don't you use blotting paper while you're at it?" he added sarcastically.

"I do," replied the Queen, "but not much."

"Very funny!" said the King. "Anyway, now you have your pepper back, so will you *please* make me the tarts?"

"Without sugar?" said the Queen.

"What's the matter, isn't the jam sweet enough?" asked the King impatiently.

"I need sugar for the dough, and my sugar has been stolen!"

"Oh, not again!" said the King wearily. "These tarts will never get made!"

Well, recovering the sugar turned out to be a relatively simple affair. The sugar was found in the house of the Duchess, and as events proved, it was stolen by either the Duchess or the Cook, but not both. They made the following statements at the trial:

DUCHESS: The cook did not steal the sugar.

COOK: The Duchess stole the sugar.

The one who stole the sugar was lying. (It is not given whether the other one lied or told the truth.)

Which one stole the sugar? Also, was the other one lying or telling the truth?

♛8

THE FIFTH TALE "Well," said the King, "here is your sugar, so you can make me the tarts."

"Without salt?" asked the Queen.

So! The salt had also been stolen! Well, this time it was found that the culprit was either the Caterpillar, Bill the Lizard, or the Cheshire Cat. (One of them had come into the kitchen and eaten up all the salt; the container wasn't missing.) The three were tried and made the following statements in court:

CATERPILLAR: Bill the Lizard ate the salt.

BILL THE LIZARD: That is true!

CHESHIRE CAT: I never ate the salt!

As it happened, at least one of them lied and at least one told the truth.

Who stole the salt?

**♛ 9**

THE SIXTH TALE "Here is some more salt, so now you can make the tarts," said the King.

"Can't," said the Queen. "Somebody stole my baking pan."

"Baking pan!" shouted the King. "Well, of course we'll have to get *that* back!"

This time the search was narrowed down to the Frog-Footman, the Fish-Footman, and the Knave of Hearts. They made the following statements at the trial:

13

FROG-FOOTMAN: It was stolen by the Fish-Footman.
FISH-FOOTMAN: Your Majesty, *I* never stole it!
KNAVE OF HEARTS: I stole it!

"A fine help *you* are!" shouted the King to the Knave. "You usually lie through your teeth!"
Well, as it happened, at most one of them lied.
Who stole the baking pan?

♛10

THE SEVENTH TALE "Here is the baking pan," said the King, "so now you can make me the tarts."
"Without a recipe?" inquired the Queen.
"Use your usual recipe," cried the King impatiently, "last time your tarts were delicious!"
"Can't," said the Queen. "The recipe is in my cookbook, and the cookbook has just been stolen!"
Well, the most likely suspect was the Duchess's Cook, and the

cookbook was indeed found in the Duchess's kitchen. The only possible suspects were the Cook, the Duchess, and the Cheshire Cat.

"The Cheshire Cat stole it!" said the Duchess at the trial.

"Oh, yes, I stole it!" said the Cheshire Cat with a grin.

"I didn't steal it!" said the Cook.

As it turned out, the thief had lied and at least one of the others had told the truth.

Who stole the cookbook?

### ♛11

THE SEVENTH TALE (CONTINUED) Shortly after the cookbook was returned to the Queen, it was stolen a second time—again by either the Duchess, the Cook, or the Cheshire Cat.

At the trial they made exactly the same statements as at the last trial. Only this time, the thief lied and the other two either both lied or both told the truth.

Who stole the cookbook this time?

### ♛12

THE EIGHTH TALE "Well, here is your cookbook back again," said the King, "so you now have the recipe. So make me the tarts!"

"Without milk, butter, or eggs?"

"Oh, me!" cried the King. "This is too much!"

"And this time I *know* it was the March Hare, the Mad Hatter, and the Dormouse," shouted the Queen, stamping her feet in rage. "I actually *saw* them sneaking out of the window when I came into the kitchen. Each was carrying something, but I couldn't tell who was carrying what."

"We'll soon settle *that!*" roared the King.

Well, the ingredients were all found at the house of the March Hare, Mad Hatter, and Dormouse. The three were tried and made the following statements at the trial:

MARCH HARE: The Hatter stole the butter.
HATTER: The Dormouse stole the eggs.
DORMOUSE: I stole the milk.

As it happened, the one who stole the butter told the truth and the one who stole the eggs lied.

Who stole what?

♛13

THE FINAL TALE "Well, here is your butter, eggs, and milk all back," said the King, "and I see you have your jam, flour, sugar, salt, baking pan, and cookbook—even your pepper. Now you can *surely* make me the tarts!"

Well, the Queen made a marvelous batch of tarts. "These are even better than last time," said the Queen to herself. "I'm sure the King will be delighted!"

The Queen went up to the Royal Chamber to announce to the King that the tarts were ready. Arm in arm they went down together to the kitchen, but when they got there, they found the table empty—the whole platter of tarts was clean gone!

"Now this has gone too far!" cried the King, paling with rage. "Who sneaks into my house like this? I've half a mind to *really* execute the culprit!"

Well, needless to say, the culprit did not really get executed, but he was caught, and the tarts were fully recovered. That ends my story.

"What do you mean, *that ends your story*?" asked (the real) Alice excitedly. "You haven't told us who stole the tarts, nor whether there was a trial, and if there was, what happened at the trial—you haven't told us *anything!*"

"Well, there was a trial," I added, "but it was a very complicated one, and for you to figure out who was guilty involves solving a complicated logic puzzle, so I think I'll wait a few years until you're all grown up, and then I'll tell you what happened."

"No, we want to know what happened!" said Tony.

"I'll let you know what happened," I replied, "but in a few more years when you're all grown up."

"No, no, we want to know *now!*" they all shouted.

"All right," I replied, "but you won't blame me if I give you a *very* complicated logic puzzle?"

"We won't blame you—really we won't. Only stop keeping us in suspense—tell us what happened!"

So I continued—

Well, as I said, the trial was quite a complicated one. The first suspect was the Knave of Hearts, but circumstantial evidence was brought forth which established beyond any reasonable doubt that the Knave of Hearts couldn't have stolen the tarts. The next suspect was the Dormouse. However, several reliable witnesses testified that

fitting

17

the Dormouse was fast asleep at the time of the robbery, hence it couldn't have been the Dormouse. At this point the trial came to a dead standstill.

Suddenly the door of the courtroom burst open, and the White Rabbit proudly entered, bearing the tray of tarts. Behind him came the soldiers, dragging in the Gryphon and the Mock Turtle in chains.

"The tarts were found on the beach," explained the White Rabbit. "The Gryphon and the Mock Turtle were just about to eat them when the soldiers happened to come by and put them in custody."

"That proves their guilt without any question of doubt," shouted the Queen, "so off with their heads immediately!"

"Now, now," said the King, "we must give them a fair trial, you know!"

Well, events happened which proved that the Gryphon and the Mock Turtle were not *both* guilty—the questions that remained were

whether either one was guilty, and if so which one; or whether someone else was guilty: Was it a mere coincidence that the tarts were found by the Gryphon and the Mock Turtle? No; evidence was soon produced that conclusively proved that either the Gryphon or the Mock Turtle was guilty (but not both), but the court could see no way to decide which one it was. It seemed that no further progress could be made, but quite suddenly a whole medley of witnesses came up, making various statements.

"The Gryphon never stole the tarts," said the Duchess.

"But he has stolen other things in the past," said the Cook.

"The Mock Turtle has stolen things in the past," said the Cheshire Cat.

"The Cheshire Cat has stolen things in the past," said the Caterpillar.

"The Cook and the Cheshire Cat are both right," said the March Hare.

"The Cook and the Caterpillar are both right," said the Dormouse.

"Either the Cheshire Cat or the Caterpillar is right—and maybe both," said the Hatter.

"Either the March Hare or the Dormouse is right—and maybe both," said Bill the Lizard.

"The Cook and the Hatter are both right," said the Knave of Hearts.

"Bill the Lizard is right and the Knave of Hearts is wrong," said the White Rabbit.

There was a dead silence.

"All this proves nothing!" roared the King. "Just words, words, words—all useless words!"

"Not so useless, your Majesty," said Alice, rising from the jury. "It so happens that the White Rabbit and the Duchess made statements which are either both true or both false."

All eyes turned eagerly to Alice. Now, everyone knew that Alice makes only true statements, and subsequent investigation showed that this statement was no exception. Moreover, this statement solved the entire mystery.

Who stole the tarts?

## CHAPTER ♛ 3

# *Who Is Mad?*

"In *that* direction," the Cat said, waving its right paw round, "lives a Hatter: and in *that* direction," waving the other paw, "lives a March Hare. Visit either you like: they're both mad."
"But I don't want to go among mad people," Alice remarked.
"Oh, you can't help that," said the Cat: "we're all mad here."

—*Alice's Adventures in Wonderland,*
CHAPTER SIX

Shortly after the trial, Alice met the Duchess, and they had the following remarkable conversation.

"The Cheshire Cat says that everyone here is mad," said Alice. "Is that really true?"

"Of course not," replied the Duchess. "If that were really true, then the Cat would also be mad, hence you could not rely on what it said."

This sounded perfectly logical to Alice.

"But I'll tell you a great secret, my dear," continued the Duchess. "*Half* the creatures around here are mad—totally mad!"

"That doesn't surprise me," said Alice, "many have seemed *quite* mad to me!"

"When I said *totally* mad," continued the Duchess, quite ignoring Alice's remark, "I meant exactly what I said: They are completely deluded! All their beliefs are wrong—not just some, but *all*. Everything true they believe to be false and everything false they believe to be true."

Alice thought awhile about this very queer state of affairs. "Does a mad person or creature believe that two plus two equals five?" asked Alice.

"Why, of course, child! Since two plus two doesn't equal five, then a mad person naturally believes that it does."

"And does a mad person also believe that two plus two equals six?"

"Of course," replied the Duchess, "since it doesn't, then the mad one believes it does."

"But it can't both equal five *and* six!" exclaimed Alice.

"Of course not," agreed the Duchess, "*you* know that and *I* know that, but a mad person doesn't. And the moral of that is—"

"What about the sane people around here?" interrupted Alice

(who had heard quite enough morals for the day). "I guess most of their beliefs are right but some of them are wrong?"

"Oh, no, no!" said the Duchess most emphatically. "That may be true where *you* come from, but around here the sane people are one hundred percent accurate in their beliefs! Everything true they know to be true and everything false they know to be false."

Alice thought this over. "Which ones around here are sane and which ones are mad?" asked Alice. "I would very much like to know this."

♛14

THE CATERPILLAR AND THE LIZARD "Well," replied the Duchess, "take, for example, the Caterpillar and Bill the Lizard. The Caterpillar believes that both of them are mad."

"Which of them is really mad?" asked Alice.

"I shouldn't have to tell you *that*!" replied the Duchess. "I have given you enough information for you to deduce the answer."

What is the solution? Is the Caterpillar mad or sane? And what about the Lizard?

♛15

THE COOK AND THE CAT "Then there's my cook and the Cheshire Cat," continued the Duchess. "The Cook believes that at least one of the two is mad."

What can you deduce about the Cook and the Cat?

♛16

THE FISH-FOOTMAN AND THE FROG-FOOTMAN "That was very interesting," said Alice. "The two cases are quite different."

"Of course they are, my dear! And the moral of that is—to be or not to be is not the same as to be *and* not to be."

Alice tried to figure out just what the Duchess had meant, when the Duchess interrupted her thoughts.

"Then there are my two footmen, the Fish-Footman and the Frog-Footman. You've met them?"

"Oh, yes, indeed!" said Alice, remembering the latter's unspeakable rudeness.

"Well, the Fish-Footman believes that he and the Frog-Footman are alike—in other words that they are either both sane or both mad. And now, my dear, it is up to *you* to tell me which ones are mad."

Alice did not quite see why it should be up to *her*. Still, the puzzle interested her, so she worked on it quite a while.

"I'm afraid I can't solve it," said Alice, "I know what one of the footmen is, but I cannot figure out the other."

"Why, you *have* solved it, you dear thing!" said the Duchess, giving Alice a hug. "The other footman *can't* be figured out from what I have told you. In fact, even *I* don't know what the other one is."

Which footman do you know to be sane or mad, and what is he?

♛17

THE KING AND QUEEN OF DIAMONDS "Then there's the King and Queen of Diamonds," began the Duchess.

"The King and Queen of Diamonds?" said Alice. "I don't believe I've met them—in fact I did not know they were around here."

"All the cards are around here," said the Duchess. "Anyway, I heard a rumor that the Queen of Diamonds was mad. However, I was not sure whether the person who told me this was mad or sane, so I decided to find out for myself.

"Well, one day I met the King of Diamonds without his Queen. I knew him to be absolutely honest, though of doubtful sanity, hence whatever he would say he would at least *believe* to be true.

"'Is your poor dear wife really mad?' I asked sympathetically."

"'She believes she is,' replied the King."

What can be deduced about the King and Queen of Diamonds?

♛18

WHAT ABOUT THESE THREE? "I've always wondered about the March Hare, the Hatter, and the Dormouse," said Alice. "The Hatter is *called* the Mad Hatter, but is he really mad? And what about the March Hare and the Dormouse?"

*24*

"Well," replied the Duchess, "the Hatter once expressed the belief that the March Hare does not believe that all three of them are sane. Also, the Dormouse believes that the March Hare is sane."

What can you deduce about these three?

### ♛19

AND THESE THREE? "Then there's the Gryphon, the Mock Turtle, and the Lobster," the Duchess began.

"I didn't know there was a real lobster around here," replied Alice. "I only know him in a poem."

"Oh, yes, there *is* a real lobster, and he is as big as the Mock Turtle," replied the Duchess. "Anyway, the Lobster once expressed the belief that the Gryphon believes that exactly one of the three is sane. The Mock Turtle believes that the Gryphon is sane."

What can you deduce about these three?

### ♛20

AND NOW, WHAT ABOUT THESE TWO? "You know," said Alice in a *very* low voice, looking around to see that the Queen of Hearts was not within hearing distance, "I am particularly interested in knowing about the King and Queen of Hearts. What are they?"

"Ah," said the Duchess, "this is an interesting story indeed! The Queen believes that the King believes that the Queen believes that the King believes that the Queen is mad."

"Now that's too much!" cried Alice. "I think *I'll* go mad if I try to puzzle that one out!"

"Very well," said the Duchess good-naturedly, "let's try an easier one first. For example, take the King and Queen of Spades."

There was a long pause.

"What about the King and Queen of Spades?" asked Alice.

"Well, the Queen believes that the King believes that she is mad. What can you tell me about the King and Queen of Spades?"

♛ 21

THE KING AND QUEEN OF CLUBS "You got that one pretty easily," said the Duchess. "Now, what would you say if I told you that the King of Clubs believes that the Queen of Clubs believes that the King of Clubs believes that the Queen of Clubs is mad?"

♛ 22

AND NOW, WHAT ABOUT THE QUEEN OF HEARTS? Alice thought this last puzzle over and said, "If you had told me that (which of course you didn't) then I'm afraid I would have had to conclude that *you* must be mad!"

"And quite right you would be!" cried the Duchess. "But of course I would never tell you any such impossible thing!

"And now," continued the Duchess, "you should be able to solve the puzzle about the King and Queen of Hearts. Remember what I told you: The Queen believes that the King believes that the Queen believes that the King believes that she is mad. The question is, Is the Queen of Hearts mad or sane?"

♛ 23

THE DODO, THE LORY, AND THE EAGLET "Then there's the Dodo, the Lory, and the Eaglet," said the Duchess. "The Dodo believes that the Lory believes that the Eaglet is mad. The Lory believes that the Dodo is mad, and the Eaglet believes that the Dodo is sane.

"Can you puzzle that out?" asked the Duchess.

♛ 24

THE KNAVE OF HEARTS  Alice solved this last puzzle.

"I think I know *why* half the people around here are mad," said Alice.

"Why?" asked the Duchess.

"I think they went mad trying to work out puzzles like *these*. They're dreadfully confusing!"

"As to *confusing* puzzles," replied the Duchess, "these are nothing compared to some I *could* tell you if I chose!"

"Oh, you needn't choose!" said Alice as politely as she could.

"For example, there's the Knave of Hearts," the Duchess went on, "he keeps company with the Spade-Gardeners, One, Two, Three, Four, Five, Six, and Seven. I believe you've met Two, Five, and Seven?"

"Oh, yes," remembered Alice, "they were having a terrible time trying to paint the white roses red, because they had by mistake planted a white rose tree in the garden instead of a red rose tree as the Queen had ordered."

"Well," said the Duchess, "Three believes that One is mad. Four believes that Three and Two are not both mad. Five believes that One and Four are either both mad or both sane. Six believes that One and Two are both sane. Seven believes that Five is mad. As for the Knave of Hearts, he believes that Six and Seven are not both mad.

"And now," continued the Duchess, "would you care to figure out whether the Knave is mad or sane, or would you prefer a more confusing puzzle?"

"Oh, no," replied poor Alice, "this one is *quite* confusing enough, thank you!"

Is the Knave of Hearts mad or sane?


♛25

THE GRYPHON'S EVALUATION "You know," said the Duchess, chuckling, "it's a funny thing—really a funny thing!"

"What is?" asked Alice.

"Why, the Cook—she thinks that *I* am mad. Isn't that a scream?"

Alice did not see why this was so funny.

"Anyway, my dear," continued the Duchess, "I must now be off to the croquet game. It was delightful talking to you again."

After the Duchess left, Alice stood quite a while in thought. She was thinking so deeply that she did not even notice the Gryphon, who had just come by.

"What you puzzling so hard?" asked the Gryphon.

Alice then told the Gryphon her entire conversation with the Duchess.

"It's all her fancy, it is," said the Gryphon, chuckling. "You can't believe *her* story, you can't."

"Why not?" asked Alice.

"Because it don't hang together, nohow—it just don't make no sense! It's just her fancy, I tells you!"

Alice thought this over. "Is it possible the Duchess was lying?" asked Alice.

"No, she wasn't lying," he replied, "she just fancied the whole story—she fancies lots of things!"

The Gryphon then explained to Alice why the Duchess's story as a whole is impossible, and he was right! If you review all the things the Duchess said, you will see that it is not consistent (assuming the Duchess was not deliberately lying).

How does one prove this?

## CHAPTER 4

# The Gryphon and the Mock Turtle

## A. The Gryphon Explains His Method

"So you sees I was right," said the Gryphon, "it was just her fancy, that's all!

"They fancies lots of things around here," continued the Gryphon. "For example, at the trial they fancied I stole them tarts, but I never stole no tarts, they only fancied I did!"

"I don't understand," said Alice. "You were found guilty, and the King sentenced you. How is it you're not in prison?"

"They don't put no peoples in prison around here," said the Gryphon, chuckling, "they only fancies they does!"

Alice puzzled a bit over this queer state of affairs.

"Anyway," continued the Gryphon, "those was nice puzzles you solved at them there trials! Now, do you know what kind of puzzles *I* takes a fancy to?"

"No," said Alice, "what kind do you like?"

"Why, the *puzzling* kind!" he answered.

"Well, of course!" said Alice. "Aren't puzzles usually puzzling?"

"Of course not!" The Gryphon laughed. "Peoples only fancies they is!"

"Well, then," asked Alice, "what would *you* call a puzzling puzzle?"

"Why, the kind peoples *fights* over," replied the Gryphon. "When peoples fights, then the fun really begins!"

"Why would people fight over a puzzle?" asked Alice.

"Oh, they does, you know! Some believes one way and some believes another. They're usually both wrong, and that's the funny part of it!

"Take here the puzzle about George and the monkey—you heard it?"

"I don't believe I have," replied Alice.

"Well, there was this here monkey standing on a hand organ. A little boy, George, wanted to tease the monkey, and so he walked around the organ. But as he walked around, the monkey kept turning and faced George the whole time. After George walked completely around the organ, had he walked around the monkey or not?"

Alice thought about this for quite a while.

"I'm really not quite sure," she replied. "Did he or didn't he?"

"I'd says he didn't," replied the Gryphon, "only others say different, they does!"

"Just what is their argument?" asked Alice.

"They says that because George walked completely around the organ, and the monkey was on top of the organ the whole time, then George's path completely encircled the monkey, therefore George must have walked around him. But I says different—I says if George had walked around the monkey, he would have seen the monkey's back. Did he see the monkey's back? No! Therefore George couldn't have walked around him nohow!"

"That's very interesting!" said Alice. "In a way I can see both points of view, and I'm not sure which one I find more convincing."

"Well, here's another," said the Gryphon.

"There was this here American dealer who sold used gadgets. A customer bought a used gadget from him for ten dollars. Soon after he bought it, the customer decided he didn't like it, so he sold it back to the dealer for eight dollars. Then comes along another customer and buys it from the dealer for nine dollars. How much profit did the dealer make?"

Alice thought about this for a while.

"Now, I gets three different answers from three different types of peoples," said the Gryphon, chuckling. "The first type tells me that the dealer made two dollars from the first customer, because he sold it to him for ten dollars and bought it back for eight dollars. But then having bought it back for eight dollars and having sold it to the second one for nine dollars, he makes another dollar. So altogether he makes three dollars on the deal.

"The second type tells me that to begin with, the gadget is worth ten dollars. Then, like the first type, he says the dealer makes two dollars off the first customer. But he then sells a ten-dollar article to the second customer for only nine dollars, so he loses one of the two dollars he had gained. So his net gain is one dollar.

"Then there's the third type, who, like the other two, tells me that the dealer made two dollars from the first customer. But when he sells the gadget to the second one for nine dollars, he has merely exchanged it for the nine dollars it is worth, so makes neither profit nor loss with the second customer. So his profit remains at two dollars.

"So," said the Gryphon, laughing, "one tells me he made three dollars, one that he made two, and one that he made one dollar. Don't you think that's funny?"

"Which of them is correct?" asked Alice.

"Why, they ain't none of 'em correct!" replied the Gryphon. "They only thinks they is, you know."

"Then what is *your* solution?" asked Alice.

"The *right* one, child, the right one!" replied the Gryphon. "There ain't but only one right way of looking at it, and it's this: You can't tell the profit nohow unless you know what the dealer paid for the gadget in the first place!"

"Will you please explain that?" asked Alice.

"Look," he said, "just what do we mean by profit? Well, when someone buys and sells something, the profit is the difference between the amount he got for the article and the amount he paid for it. So, if I was to sell you something for nine dollars for which I

paid seven dollars, I would make a profit of two dollars. Could anything be clearer than that?"

"No," replied Alice, "that seems correct to me."

"*Seems*, child? Nay, it is!" replied the Gryphon. "So this here dealer took in eleven dollars—he first took in ten, then gave out eight, leaving two, then took in another nine, so that makes eleven. Therefore the dealer would have done the same moneywise if instead of these three deals, he had had only one customer and sold the gadget outright for eleven dollars. Right?"

"Yes," replied Alice, "I see that."

"Then obviously the dealer's profit was eleven dollars minus whatever the dealer paid for the gadget. Could anything be clearer than that?"

"No," said Alice, "I agree with you completely."*

The Gryphon certainly seems to know his arithmetic, thought Alice, and his thinking is remarkably logical. If only his *English* weren't so atrocious!

"What you thinking?" asked the Gryphon.

Alice was a little startled by this interruption of her thoughts.

"I was thinking," replied Alice, as politely as she could, "that you are very good at arithmetic."

"I know I is!" said the Gryphon. "Here—let me try you on another. You know the puzzle about the raspberry tarts?"

"You mean the stolen tarts?" asked Alice.

"Oh, no, not *those!*" quickly replied the Gryphon, who was not at all eager to speak about *that* subject! "I meant *different* tarts altogether!"

"Then I don't think I know it," replied Alice.

"Well, you see," the March Hare and the Hatter were having this here tea party—"

"What about the Dormouse?" Alice inquired.

"The Dormouse was fast asleep the whole time, so he don't figure in this puzzle. Anyway, the two were having raspberry tarts with their tea. Now, the Hatter had three times as many tarts as the March Hare, and the March Hare didn't like this."

---

*This puzzle is a variant of a famous old puzzle of the American Sam Lloyd.

"I don't blame him!" remarked Alice.

"Anyway, the Hatter begrudgingly gave one of his tarts to the March Hare. 'That's not enough!' cried the March Hare angrily. 'You still have twice as many as I do!' Now, the problem is, How many more tarts must the Hatter give the March Hare so that they each have the same amount?"

"How many tarts were there altogether?" asked Alice.

"I'm not telling you that!" cried the Gryphon. "That would make it way too easy!"

Alice thought it strange that the puzzle could be solved without knowing how many tarts there were, but she determined to try. She thought for a while, and then shook her head.

"I'm afraid I can't do this one. I'm sure if my sister were here she could—she's older than I, you know, and she has learned algebra. I'm sure with algebra this could be done."

"You don't needs no algebra!" The Gryphon laughed. "It's only your fancy you does!"

"Well, the only way I can think of doing it is by trial and error—trying until I finally guess the right number of tarts."

"You don't needs no guessing!" said the Gryphon. "You don't needs no guessing and you don't needs no algebra neither! Now, I know that in the schools they teaches you to do this sort of thing with algebra, but I haven't been much to no schools, so I figured out my own method—and it's every bit as good as those they learn you!"

"Really?" said Alice. "I'd be *very* interested in seeing your method. What is it?"

"Well," said the Gryphon, "your first question was the right one: How many tarts were there altogether?"

"I can see now," replied Alice, "that if I knew *that*, the rest would be easy."

"Right," said the Gryphon. "Now, to figure out how many tarts there must be, here's how I sees it: To begin with, the Hatter had three times as many as the March Hare, which means that he had three parts of the tarts to the March Hare's one part—in other words he had three out of four parts, so he started out with three-quarters of the tarts."

"That's right," said Alice, "he had three-quarters and the March

Hare had one-quarter, and since three-quarters is three times as much as one-quarter, the Hatter did indeed have three times as much as the March Hare to start with."

"Good," said the Gryphon. "Now then, after he gave the March Hare one tart, he had twice as many tarts as the March Hare. What fraction of all the tarts did he then have?"

"Let's see," said Alice. "Reasoning the same way, he had two parts to the March Hare's one part—in other words, he had two tarts to every one of the March Hare's, or, out of every three tarts, the Hatter had two and the March Hare had one. This means that the Hatter had two-thirds of the tarts and the March Hare had one-third."

"Quite right," said the Gryphon.

"Well, where do we go from there?" asked Alice.

"Ah," said the Gryphon, "the whole point is that by giving the March Hare just one tart, the Hatter reduced his share from three-quarters to two-thirds. Now, how much reduction is that? In other words, what fraction of the tarts when taken away from three-quarters leaves two-thirds?"

"I'm not sure I understand you," replied Alice.

"What I'm really asking is how much is three-quarters minus two-thirds? That's the amount needed to take away from three-quarters to get two-thirds!"

"Oh, I understand!" said Alice. "Let's see now, three-quarters minus two-thirds? I think we better first reduce everything to twelfths."

"You sure better!" replied the Gryphon.

"Well, three-quarters is nine-twelfths, and two-thirds is eight-twelfths, so the difference is one-twelfth."

"Right," said the Gryphon. "And now can you solve the puzzle?"

"I *still* don't see how!" replied Alice.

"Then you've missed the whole point!" replied the Gryphon. "The point is that by giving the March Hare one tart, he gave him one-twelfth of the total number of tarts. So one tart is one-twelfth the number of tarts. Therefore—"

"Therefore there were twelve tarts!" interrupted Alice excitedly. "That means the Hatter originally had nine—which is three-quarters of twelve—and the March Hare had three—and nine *is* three times as much as three! Then the Hatter gave one to the March Hare, which left eight for the Hatter, and the March Hare had four, so the Hatter then had twice as many as the March Hare. So twelve *is* the right number!"

"What about the rest of the puzzle?" asked the Gryphon.

"Oh, yes!" remembered Alice. "Well, at this stage the Hatter has eight and the March Hare has four. Now, they finally have the same number, which must be six. So the Hatter has got to give two more tarts to the March Hare. So the answer to the puzzle is *two.*"

"Bravo!" said the Gryphon. "You see, I was right; you didn't need no algebra!"

"This is extremely interesting," said Alice. "Could you give me another?"

⚜26

HOW MANY? "Now that's what I call a good pupil!" said the Gryphon. "Surely I'll give you another. The principle is now a little different, but I'm sure you'll get it.

"This time the Hatter, the March Hare, and the Dormouse are all having a tea party together, and the Dormouse is quite awake, and also wants some tarts. Well, the Hatter had already set the places, and had given himself three times as many tarts as he had given the March Hare, and the Dormouse had been given only half as many as the March Hare."

"The poor Dormouse really had the worst of the bargain!" said Alice sympathetically.

"Decidedly!" replied the Gryphon. "Anyway, the Hatter had twenty more tarts than the Dormouse."

"That's an *enormous* number of tarts!" said Alice.

"Not really," replied the Gryphon, "because the tarts were *extremely* small. Anyway, how many tarts did each one have?

"And you don't need no algebra!" he added.

What is the solution?

## ☛ 27

THE TABLES ARE TURNED! "The Hatter always seems to get the best of the bargain!" remarked Alice.

"Usually, yes," replied the Gryphon, "but on one occasion, the other two got even! On this occasion, the Hatter had set the places, and put *all* the tarts on his own plate—he left nothing for the March Hare or the Dormouse. Now the table was set out on the lawn, and when the Hatter went into the house to brew the tea, the March Hare quickly took five-sixteenths of the tarts from the plate and ate them. Then the Dormouse ate up seven-elevenths of the remaining tarts. This left eight tarts for the Hatter. How many tarts did each of the other two eat?"

## ☛ 28

HOW MANY FAVORITES? "Here's a slightly different kind of puzzle," said the Gryphon. "One day the Queen of Hearts was entertaining thirty guests. She had one hundred tarts to divide among them. Rather than cut any tart in pieces, she decided to give four tarts apiece to each of her favorites, and three apiece to each of the other guests. How many favorites did she have?"

♛ 29

LARGE TARTS AND SMALL TARTS "Here's another," said the Gryphon. "The Hatter had to go out shopping one day for the next tea party.

"'How much are your tarts?' he asked the shopkeeper.

"'Depends on the size; we have small ones and large ones. A large one costs the same as three small ones.'

"'How much would it cost me to buy seven large ones and four small ones?' asked the March Hare.

"'Twelve cents more than if you bought four large ones and seven small ones,' was the enigmatic reply.

"How much does a large tart cost?"

♛ 30

THE VISIT "Here's a nice one," said the Gryphon. "One day the Hatter, the March Hare, and the Dormouse went over to visit the Duchess, the Cook, and the Cheshire Cat. When they got there, no one was home. A batch of tarts was lying on the kitchen table. First the Hatter helped himself to half of the tarts, and then decided to eat one more. Then the March Hare ate half of what was left and one more. Then the Dormouse ate half of what was left and one more. Just then the Cheshire Cat came in and ate half of what was left and one more. This finished off the tarts. How many tarts were there?"

♛ 31

HOW MANY DAYS DID HE WORK? "Here's one," said the Gryphon. "It's usually solved with algebra; only if you use my method, you don't need no algebra!

"One day the King of Hearts hired one of the Spade-Gardeners for twenty-six days to do some work in the garden. The King stipulated in advance that for every day the gardener worked, he would receive three tarts, but for every day the gardener was idle, he got no tarts, but instead had to pay the King one tart."

A thought occurred to Alice. "Suppose the gardener were idle enough days so that he would end up owing the King some tarts, and he didn't have any to give the King. What would happen then?"

"Then he would get executed, of course!"

"But I thought you once said that they never execute people around here."*

"Of course they doesn't." The Gryphon grinned. "But they *says* they does, and that's enough to scare 'em, you know!

"Anyway," continued the Gryphon, "the gardener ended up earning sixty-two tarts. How many days did he work?"

"You certainly seem interested in *tarts!*" said Alice, looking intently at the Gryphon.

"Now, look here, miss," said the Gryphon, "if you're still thinking about that trial, I already told you I never stole them tarts—they only fancied I did!"

"I still don't understand how you escaped going to prison!" said Alice.

"I had my own little private talk with the King after the trial," the Gryphon explained.

*The Gryphon said this in *Alice's Adventures in Wonderland.*

This explanation did not quite satisfy Alice.

"Suppose we changes the subject," said the Gryphon, "we've talked enough about tarts! Here, let me tell you a good puzzle about the Royal clocks."

 32

WHAT TIME WAS IT? "What is the puzzle about the Royal clocks?" asked Alice.

"Well, you see, the King of Hearts has his clock, and the Queen of Hearts has hers. They both chime on the hour. The King's clock chimes faster than the Queen's—in fact, the King's clock makes three chimes in the same time that the Queen's clock makes two. One day, at a certain hour, the two clocks started chiming at the same time. After the King's clock finished chiming, the Queen's clock made two more chimes. At what time did this occur?"

## B. The Mock Turtle Joins In

"I liked that puzzle," said Alice. "It was simple but pleasant. I like puzzles about time."

"Then let me tell you my best one!" said the Gryphon. "—Hey, speak about time, here comes the Mock Turtle, and he certainly seems to be taking all day about it!"

Alice looked up, and there indeed was the Mock Turtle slowly advancing toward them, sighing and sobbing as he came.

"Why is he *always* so sad?" asked Alice.

"I already told you, he ain't got no real sorrow—he only fancies he does!" replied the Gryphon.

"Hey, old thing," said the Gryphon, when the Mock Turtle finally reached them, "you know lots of puzzles—tell this here lady some— she likes them sorts of things, she do!"

The Mock Turtle made no reply, but only sighed more deeply and hid his face in his paws.

"What's the matter, you deaf?" said the Gryphon. "Tell us a puzzle, I says!"

"I—I—can't!" sobbed the Mock Turtle.

"Why not, you dumb or something?"

"It's just—it's just that—"

"It's just that *what?*" asked the Gryphon.

"It's just that—it's just that—that they're so sad!" sobbed the Mock Turtle.

"Oh, come off it!" said the Gryphon. "Just tell us one and let *us* judge whether it's so sad. And don't be all day about it!"

"Well," said the Mock Turtle, "I know one very sad one, but it's also very beautiful!"

##### ♛33

HOW MANY WERE LOST? Alice and the Gryphon had to wait several minutes before the Mock Turtle could compose himself sufficiently to continue.

"You see," said the Mock Turtle—

"I don't see!" replied the Gryphon.

The Mock Turtle made no immediate reply, but only buried his face in his paws again. After some time, he continued.

"Let's put it this way—there were nine men lost in the mountains. They had food enough to last only five days. Just think of it, *only five days!*"

At this point the Mock Turtle was so overcome by the tragedy of the situation that he just could not continue.

"There, there!" the Gryphon said consolingly, as he patted the Mock Turtle on the back.

"Just think what will happen if they're not rescued!" sobbed the Mock Turtle. "However—and now comes the beautiful part of the story! The beautiful part," the Mock Turtle continued, "is that the next day they met another party of lost men."

"What's so beautiful about that?" asked the Gryphon.

"Well," replied the Mock Turtle, "the beautiful part is that the nine men generously shared their provisions with the other lost men—they divided the food equally, and the food lasted three more days. How many men were in the second party?"

☙ 34

HOW MUCH WATER WAS SPILLED? "What did finally happen to these men?" Alice asked a bit anxiously, after having solved the puzzle.

"Oh, they were all finally rescued," replied the Mock Turtle.

"Then what's so sad about the story?" asked Alice.

"Just think," said the Mock Turtle, "it *could* have happened that they weren't rescued!"

"Oh," said the Gryphon, "so in other words it *could* have been a sad story, but actually it wasn't!"

"It's a very sad story!" said the Mock Turtle, sobbing again.

"Come on, tell us another!" said the Gryphon.

"Well," said the Mock Turtle, "this time a shipwrecked crew had just enough water to last thirteen days, allowing each man one quart a day. On the fifth day, some water was accidentally spilled, and one man died on the same day. The water then lasted just the expected time. How much water was spilled?"

☙ 35

WHEN WILL HE GET OUT OF PRISON? "That *was* a sad one," Alice admitted, after she had solved the puzzle, "and it was also very interesting! Do you have another?"

"Well," said the Mock Turtle, "a man was once sent to prison. To make his punishment even worse, he was not told how long he would have to remain in prison."

"That was *most* unfair!" exclaimed Alice indignantly.

"It sure was!" said the Gryphon.

"Anyway," continued the Mock Turtle, "his gaoler was a very decent sort of chap, and took a liking to the prisoner.

"'Come on now,' pleaded the prisoner to the gaoler, 'can't you give me a *little* hint how long I'll have to stay in this place?'

"'How old are you?' asked the gaoler.

"'I'm twenty-five,' replied the prisoner.

"'And I'm fifty-four,' said the gaoler. 'Tell me, on what day were you born?'

"'Today is my birthday,' replied the prisoner.

"'Remarkable!' said the gaoler. 'It's also mine! Well, if it's any help to you, I'll tell you—not that I should, you know, but I will—I'll tell you that on the day I'm exactly twice as old as you—on that day, you'll get out.'

"How long does the prisoner have to serve?"

"That was a nice puzzle!" said Alice, after she solved it. "Only one thing I'd like to know: Why was the prisoner sent to gaol?"

"He stole some tarts from the King," the Mock Turtle replied.

The Gryphon looked *extremely* uncomfortable at this point, and started scratching himself furiously!

"Come on, tell us a better one!" roared the Gryphon, "and make it about something *completely* different!"

☙ 36

HOW LONG TO GET OUT? "Well, there's the one about the frog who fell into a well," began the Mock Turtle.

"Aw, come on! That puzzle has whiskers on it," said the Gryphon. "Don't you know any *new* ones?"

"I haven't heard that one," remarked Alice.

"All right, I'll tell you what you does," said the Gryphon, with a yawn, "you tells this here puzzle to the lady who ain't heard it, and

I'll meanwhile take a nap. Only I wants you to wake me when you're through, you hear?"

The Gryphon then coiled himself into a perfect position for a nap, while the Mock Turtle told Alice this old puzzle of the frog.

"One morning a frog fell into a well thirty feet deep. By day he could climb up three feet, but each night he slipped back two feet. How many days did it take the frog to get out of the well?"

### ♛ 37

DID HE CATCH THE TRAIN? "Now, wasn't that puzzle sad?" asked the Mock Turtle, "—that poor frog being in the well all those days and having to make such an arduous climb to get out!"

"Aw, shucks!" said the Gryphon, "the saddest part of that puzzle is that I heard you the whole time and couldn't sleep nohow! Come on, tell us another!"

"Well," said the Mock Turtle, "a man once had to go by bicycle twelve miles to the railroad station to catch a train. He reasoned in the following manner: 'I have an hour and a half to catch the train. Four miles is uphill, which I must walk, and can do it four miles an hour; there are four miles downhill, where I can coast at twelve miles an hour; and there are four miles of level road, which I shall do at eight miles an hour. This is an average of eight miles an hour, so I will be just in time.' Was his reasoning correct?"

### ♛ 38

WHAT ABOUT THIS ONE? "That poor man," sobbed the Mock Turtle, "just think—if he had been a little more clever, he could have left earlier and made the train!

"I'm reminded of another," continued the Mock Turtle. "A train started from a station eleven minutes late, and went at ten miles an hour to the next station, which is one and a half miles away, and where it stops for fourteen and a half minutes. A man reached the first station twelve minutes after the train was scheduled to leave and walked to the next station at four miles an hour, hoping to catch the train there. Did he succeed?"

♛ 39

HOW FAR AWAY IS THE SCHOOL? The Mock Turtle was weeping bitterly the whole time that Alice and the Gryphon were solving the last puzzle.

"Now, what's so sad about *that*?" yelled the Gryphon angrily. "The guy caught the train, didn't he?"

"Ye-es," admitted the Mock Turtle, "but we don't know what happened after that! For all we know, the train might have gotten wrecked!"

"Now, really!" said Alice. "At that rate you can make a sad story out of anything!"

The Mock Turtle made no reply to this, but once again buried his face in his paws.

"All right, here's another sad one," he said at last. "One morning a boy had to go to school—"

"Ah, that *is* sad!" admitted the Gryphon.

"No, no, *that's* not the sad part," said the Mock Turtle, "the sad part is yet to come!"

Alice and the Gryphon listened attentively for the sad part, but were unable to discover it.

"Now," continued the Mock Turtle, "the father said to the boy, 'You better hurry up or you'll be late for school!' The boy replied, 'Oh, I know exactly what I am doing: If I walk at the rate of four miles an hour, I'll be five minutes late, but if I walk at five miles an hour, I'll be ten minutes early.'

"How far away was the school?"

♔40

IS THIS PUZZLE SAD? "What was so sad about that?" asked Alice.

"It's a long way to have to walk to school every morning!" replied the Mock Turtle.

"Aw, it probably did him good!" said the Gryphon. "That's the trouble with children nowadays—they're too lazy!"

"Here's another sad puzzle," said the Mock Turtle. "An American art dealer one day sold two paintings for nine hundred and ninety dollars each. On one he made a ten percent profit and on the other he took a ten percent loss. 'That means I broke even today,' he said to himself.

"Is there anything sad about this puzzle?"

## C. The Gryphon's Prize Puzzle

"Now let me tell *you* both a puzzle," said the Gryphon. "It's my prize puzzle!"

"Is it very sad?" asked the Mock Turtle.

"No, it's not one bit sad!" said the Gryphon. "It's just clever, that's all!"

"Where did you get it?" asked Alice.

"I made it up myself—it's the one I was going to tell you before."

"Oh, good!" said Alice.

⬥41

WHO IS OLDER? "The puzzle is about the March Hare and the Hatter. One of them was born in the year 1842, but I won't tell you which one. The other one was born either in 1843 or 1844; but again, I won't tell you which. Also, the March Hare was born in March—did you know that?"

"No," said Alice, "but I'm not surprised."

"Neither am I," said the Mock Turtle.

"Anyway," continued the Gryphon, "the March Hare has a watch that . . ."

"Oh yes," interrupted Alice, "a very funny watch that tells the day of the month instead of the hour of the day. I've seen it."

"Not *that* watch," cried the Gryphon, "he has another watch that tells the hour of the day like ordinary watches do. The Hatter also has his own watch. Neither watch keeps perfect time; the Hatter's watch gains ten seconds every hour and the March Hare's watch loses ten seconds every hour.

"One day in January they put both watches right at exactly twelve o'clock noon. 'You realize,' said the Hatter, 'that our watches won't be together again until your next birthday—the day you will be twenty-one.'

"'Quite right,' replied the March Hare.

"Who is older, the March Hare or the Hatter?"

"Beats me!" said the Mock Turtle, who slowly walked away.

"Now really!" exclaimed Alice. "This puzzle can actually be solved?"

"Oh, yes!" replied the Gryphon.

What is the solution?

CHAPTER ♛ 5

# The King's Story

Of all the puzzle-adventures in Wonderland, those that now follow are the ones Alice liked best. Not till her later journey through the Looking-Glass did Alice come across such remarkable examples of logical reasoning.

That last puzzle of the Gryphon was really good! thought Alice, after she had left the Gryphon and the Mock Turtle. I wonder why the Mock Turtle thought his puzzles were so sad. I think he was being overly sentimental!

Alice walked quite a long way and after a while came across the King of Hearts, seated all by himself on a bench, totally lost in thought. Alice stood by for a while, not daring to say anything to disturb him. Kings *sometimes* think about important things, thought Alice. At least, so I have been told—so it would never do for *me* to begin the conversation!

After some time, the King noticed Alice's presence and smiled.

"That was very fine work you did at the trials," he said. "You displayed great sagacity for one so young!"

Alice was not quite sure whether she knew the word sagacity, but whatever it *did* mean, it somehow *sounded* nice and was evidently meant as a compliment—at least judging from the King's expression and tone of voice.

"Oh, I enjoyed the trials enormously," said Alice, "and I certainly wish to thank you for allowing me to serve on the jury."

"Now, that Gryphon—he nearly got away with the tarts, didn't he?" said the King with a sly grin.

"Oh, yes," replied Alice. "As a matter of fact, I saw the Gryphon a short while ago, and I was wondering why—"

"Oh, that!" interrupted the King, who had guessed Alice's question. "Well, you see, some time ago the Gryphon performed a very valuable service for me—one that nearly saved my life!"

"Just a minute," interrupted Alice. "What do you mean *nearly* saved your life? You seem fully alive to me—and, happily, in the best of health!"

"Quite right," replied the King. "Anyway, out of gratitude, I decided to pardon the Gryphon shortly after I sentenced him.

"Besides," the King continued, "he hadn't actually *eaten* any of the tarts, you know. If he had, I'm not so sure I would have been quite so generous!"

Ah, that finally explains it, thought Alice.

"And now," continued the King, "you were doubtless wondering what I was thinking about when you came by?"

"Yes, to tell the truth, I was a bit curious."

"It's always good to tell the truth," replied the King. "Well, all my life I've been interested in logic and law. And I was thinking about some remarkable cases I read in a book—oh, ever so long ago! It is a

very old book—I don't think I've seen it since I was a boy. I lost the book a long time ago, but I remember the cases as clearly as if it were yesterday!"

"This sounds interesting!" said Alice.

"The most interesting part was the last chapter," continued the King. "It was all about trials of secret agents—sometimes known as *spies*. The chapter started out with some very simple cases and ended up with the best puzzle I've ever heard in my life!"

Alice was getting more and more curious.

"I can give you a verbatim account of the whole chapter, if you like!"

"Oh, I certainly *would* like to hear it!" exclaimed Alice.

"Very well then," said the King. "All the cases take place in a land far, far away—a very strange land inhabited exclusively by knights who always tell the truth, and knaves who always lie—"

"Oh, I know those puzzles!" said Alice.

"Now, I declare," said the King quite angrily, "you should never say you *know* those puzzles until you have heard what the puzzles are! There are countless puzzles about liars and truth-tellers, child, and the odds are a million to one you don't know *these* puzzles!

"You remind me," continued the King, still vividly agitated, "of those children who, when they see a magician take out a pack of cards, about to entertain them with some conjuring tricks, say 'I know that trick!' Why, there are countless tricks which can be done with a pack of cards—just as there are countless puzzles that can be told about knights who always tell the truth and knaves who always lie. The book was old and extremely rare even in my early days, and I doubt there are any copies left at all! So, as I said, the odds are a million to one against your knowing any of these puzzles."

I wonder where the King got those exact odds, thought Alice. Still, she was a *little* ashamed of her hastiness and decided not to interrupt the King again any more than necessary.

﹌42

ENTER THE FIRST SPY "Now, then," said the King, "as I said, the knights of this land always told the truth—they never lied—and the knaves of this land always lied—they never told the truth. One day there was great excitement in the land, because it was known that a spy had entered from another land."

"How was it known?" asked Alice, quite forgetting her resolution.

"I have no idea," replied the King, "and it happens to be *most* irrelevant to the problem!"

"Did the spy lie or tell the truth?" asked Alice.

"Ah, that's what complicated matters!" replied the King. "The spy was neither a knight nor a knave; he sometimes told the truth and sometimes lied—he always did what most suited his convenience.

"It was known that the spy was living with two other inhabitants and that one of them was a knight and the other a knave. The officers arrested all three one day but didn't know which one was the knight, which one was the knave, and which one was the spy. Let us call these three A, B, and C.

"At the interrogation, A claimed that C was a knave, and B claimed that A was a knight. Then C was asked what he was, and C replied, 'I am the spy.'"

Which one was the spy, which one was the knight, and which one was the knave?

☙ 43

THE CASE OF THE BUNGLING SPY "That wasn't too difficult," said Alice, after she had solved the problem.

"They get more difficult later on," replied the King. "The book was well written and slowly progressed from the more easy to the more difficult. The next two puzzles are also rather easy—still, they make one think.

"Well, the spy was sent to gaol, but soon after, another spy enered the land. The officers made an arrest one day, but they weren't sure whether their man was a spy or not. Actually, the man was a spy, but the officers didn't know it. The spy was brought in for questioning and was asked to make a statement. He then made a false statement, but it was a very stupid thing for him to have done, because it immediately convicted him."

Can you supply such a statement?

### ♛ 44

ANOTHER BUNGLING SPY "The spy was sent to prison, of course," said the King, "but then another spy entered the land. The officers arrested him, but were not sure whether he was a spy. This time the spy made a true statement, but was again very foolish in having done so, for the statement convicted him."

Can you supply such a statement?

### ♛ 45

THE CASE OF THE FOXY SPY "The next spy who entered the land," said the King, "was far more clever! He was arrested one day together with two others, one of whom was a knight and the other a knave. The case was brought to trial. The court knew that one was a knight, one a knave, and the other a spy (who sometimes lies and sometimes tells the truth), but the court didn't know who was which. Again, we will call the three defendants A, B, and C.

"First A said, 'I am not a spy.' Then B said, 'I am a spy.' Then C was asked, 'Is B really a spy?'

"Now, it so happened that C was the spy. Being a spy, he can either lie or tell the truth as he chooses. Well, he did the foxiest thing possible and answered in such a way as not to convict himself."

What did he answer?

☙46

WHO IS MURDOCH? "Another spy by the name of Murdoch entered the land. He is one of A, B, C, and one of the three is a knight and the other a knave. The spy is the only one of the three named Murdoch. The three made the following statements in court:

A: My name is Murdoch.
B: That is true.
C: I am Murdoch.

Which one is the spy?

☙47

THE RETURN OF MURDOCH "Well," continued the King, "Murdoch was sent to prison, but soon after, he escaped and fled the land. He then came back well disguised, so no one could recognize him. Again, he was arrested in the company of a knight and a knave, and the three—call them A, B, C—made the following statements at the trial:

A: My name is Murdoch.
B: That is true.
C: I am not Murdoch.

Which one is Murdoch this time?

**♛ 48**

A MORE INTERESTING CASE "And now, we come to the more interesting cases," said the King.

Alice was all ears.

"Well," began the King, "in this trial we again have three defendants—A, B, C. The court knew that one was a knight, one a knave, and the other the spy, but it was not known who was which. First A accused B of being the spy; then B accused C of being the spy; and then C pointed to one of the other two defendants and said, 'He is really the spy!' The judge then convicted the spy. Which one did he convict?"

"Now, just a minute," cried Alice. "You don't expect me to solve this without your telling me which one C pointed to, do you?"

"When I read this case in the book," replied the King, "I also thought that not enough information was given to solve it. But when I thought a bit more deeply about it, I realized there was. Yes, enough information *has* been given to determine the solution."

Which one was the spy?

**♛ 49**

A STILL MORE INTERESTING CASE "And now, we come to a more interesting case yet," said the King. "Again we have three defendants—A, B, and C. The court knew that one was a knight, one a knave, and one the spy, but it was not known who was which.

First the judge asked A, 'Are you the spy?' A answered (yes or no). Then the judge asked B, 'Did A tell the truth?' B answered (again either yes or no).

"At this point, A said, 'C is not the spy.' The judge replied, 'I already knew that. And now I know who the spy is!'

"Who was the spy?"

"Now, just a minute!" cried Alice. "This time you haven't told me what either A or B said!"

"I know," replied the King. "The book didn't tell us that either, but the interesting thing is that it is possible to identify the spy without being told either of those things."

Alice continued to look puzzled.

"You realize," said the King, "that when the judge said that he already knew that C was not the spy, it was purely on the basis of the answers given by A and B."

What is the solution?

### ⚜ 50

AN EQUALLY INTERESTING CASE "In this equally interesting case," continued the King, "the court again knew of the three defendants A, B, C, that one was a knight, one a knave, and one a spy.

"The judge said, 'I shall ask a series of questions—all answers must be yes or no. If, at any point, I have identified the spy, I shall convict him, and the case will be terminated. If, at any point, I know of any of you that he is definitely not the spy, then I shall acquit him before proceeding further.'

"The judge then asked A, 'Are you the spy?' A answered. The judge then asked B, 'Did A tell the truth?' B answered. The judge thought for a while and then asked C, 'Are you the spy?' C answered, and the judge made a conviction. Who was the spy?"

"Now, just a minute!" exclaimed Alice excitedly. "Do you realize that you haven't told me one single thing that *any* of the defendants said?"

"True," replied the King, "but the problem is solvable, nevertheless."

What is the solution?

**♛ 51**

THE MOST INTERESTING CASE OF ALL "And now, we come to the prize problem," said the King. "A certain Mr. Anthony attended a spy trial in which at the outset the court knew of the three defendants, A, B, C, that one of them was a knight, one a knave, and one a spy. The judge first asked A, 'Are you a spy?' A answered yes or no. Then B was asked, 'Did A tell the truth?' B answered yes or no, and the judge then pointed to one of the three defendants and said, 'You are not the spy, so you may leave the court.' The man gladly did this. The judge then asked one of the two remaining defendants whether the other one was a spy. The defendant answered yes or no, and the judge then knew who the spy was.

"Now," continued the King, "it is not yet possible for *you* to know who the spy was—there is more to come. Well, Mr. Anthony told this case to a friend who was a barrister. The friend worked on the problem awhile and said, 'I don't have enough information to solve

this case. Could you at least tell me whether the judge got the same answer to all three questions?' Mr. Anthony told him. It is not given whether or not the friend was then able to solve the problem.

"Then Mr. Anthony told the same problem to a second friend who was also a barrister. The second friend wanted to know whether or not the judge got at least two *no* answers. Mr. Anthony told him. Whether or not the second friend was able to solve the problem is not given.

"What is given," continued the King, "is that either both friends solved the problem, or neither solved the problem, but we are not told which.

"And now," concluded the King, "*your* problem is, Who was the spy?"

"It is *really* possible to solve this?" cried Alice in amazement.

"Yes," replied the King, "I can solemnly assure you it is!"

"It is *really* possible to solve this?" cried Alice in amazement (not the Alice in Wonderland, but the Alice of the party at which I was telling the story).

"Yes," I replied, "I can assure you it is."

"How come you don't *solemnly* assure us like the King?" asked Tony.

"Well," I replied with a laugh, "I'm not a king, you know—and also, I'm not really the solemn type!

"Anyhow," I continued, "the puzzle really does have a solution, though it takes a good deal of thought to get it; it is more subtle than any other puzzle I have yet given you. This is a puzzle I will leave with you, and when I get back to town, we can discuss it further."

"You are going away?" asked Tony.

"My wife and I have to leave for several weeks," I replied, "but we'll be back later in the summer. Then maybe we can all get together again and have some more fun."

# Part II

# LOOKING-GLASS LOGIC

## CHAPTER 6

# *The Twelfth Question*

Tony's birthday was later in the summer, and my wife and I got back in time for the party.

"How about some more Alice in Wonderland puzzles?" asked Alice.

"How about Alice in the Looking-Glass?" I asked.

"Either is fine with me!" replied Alice.

The children were all amenable to *any* more Alice puzzles, so I told them the following stories.

"I do think it high time the child takes another examination don't you?" the Red Queen asked the White Queen.

"Absolutely!" replied the White Queen.

Alice could not see just *why* she should have to take another examination, nor did she particularly *like* the idea, yet she made no reply.

"Can you count?" asked the Red Queen.

"Why, of course!" replied Alice.

"Very well then, let's see if you can really count. Are you ready?"

"I'm ready," said Alice.

"A stagecoach went from London to Harwich and started out with six passengers. Do you think you can remember that?"

"Of course I can remember that," replied Alice. "There's not much to remember!"

"Very well," replied the Queen, "the coach made a stop and two passengers got off and four passengers got on. Got that?"

"Yes," replied Alice, who was keeping count.

"Then the coach went on, made another stop, and three passengers got off. Are you following?"

"Yes," said Alice, who was still faithfully keeping count.

"Then the coach went on, made another stop, and two passengers got off and two passengers got on."

"That's the same as if the coach hadn't stopped at all!" exlaimed Alice.

"I wish you wouldn't keep interrupting me!" exclaimed the Red Queen. "It only puts me out!"

"I haven't *kept* interrupting you," replied Alice (who is very logical). "I've interrupted you only once, and one must interrupt someone at least twice before he can be said to *keep* interrupting him."

"True," replied the Queen, "but *I'm* giving this examination, child, not *you!*

"Anyway," continued the Queen, "the coach went on, made another stop, and three people got off and five got on. Are you still keeping count?"

"Yes, I am," replied Alice.

"Then the coach arrived in Harwich and all the passengers got off. How many times did the coach stop?"

"Oh, I wasn't counting *that!*" exclaimed Alice.

"You see, she can't count!" the Red Queen triumphantly exclaimed.

"Not a bit!" the White Queen agreed.

"You'll never be able to pass an examination unless you can count!" said the Red Queen.

"But I *can* count," pleaded poor Alice. "It's just that I counted the wrong thing!"

"That's no excuse," replied the Red Queen. "You should always count everything, because everything counts."

Alice tried to puzzle this out, and the Red Queen continued, "Now, here are the rules of the examination. We will ask you twelve questions, and you are allowed at most three wrong answers in order to pass."

And so the examination began.

### ♛ 52

THE FIRST QUESTION "Do you know how to divide?" asked the Red Queen.

"Why, of course!" replied Alice.

"Very well then, suppose you divide eleven thousand eleven hundred and eleven by three. What remainder do you get? You may use this pencil and paper if you like."

Alice set to work and made a calculation.

"I get a remainder of two," replied Alice.

"Wrong!" exclaimed the Red Queen triumphantly. "You see, she can't do division!"

"Not a bit!" agreed the White Queen.

Why don't you try this puzzle with pencil and paper, and see if Alice was right? Then you better read the solution!

### ♛ 53

ANOTHER DIVISION "Let's try another division," said the Red Queen. "How much is a million divided by a quarter?"

"Why, a quarter of a million, of course!" replied Alice, "in other words, two hundred and fifty thousand.

"Oh, no!" Alice suddenly realized. "I meant—"

"Too late to change your mind!" said the Red Queen.

Did Alice pass or fail this problem?

♛ 54

HOW MUCH? "She can't do division one bit!" repeated the Red Queen. "Shall I try her on addition and subtraction?"

"Absolutely!" replied the White Queen.

"All right," said the Red Queen, "a bottle of wine cost thirty shillings. The wine cost twenty-six shillings more than the bottle. How many shillings is the bottle worth?"

Alice got this one right. Can you?

♛ 55

AWAKE OR ASLEEP? "Here is a logic question," said the White Queen. "Whenever the Red King is asleep, everything he believes is wrong. In other words, everything the Red King believes in his sleep is false. On the other hand, everything he believes while he is awake is true. Well, last night at ten o'clock sharp, the Red King believed that both he and the Red Queen were asleep at that time. Was the Red Queen asleep or awake at the time?"

Alice thought this over, and at first believed the situation was impossible. But she suddenly realized that the situation was not impossible and was able to figure out the answer.

What is the answer?

### ⚜56

AWAKE OR ASLEEP? "I am like the Red King," said the Red Queen. "I also believe only false things when I am asleep, and I believe only true things when I am awake. Now, the night before last at eleven o'clock, the Red King believed I was asleep. At the same time, I either believed that he was asleep or I believed that he was awake. Which did I believe?"

Alice had to think rather hard to get this one, but she finally did. What is the solution?

### ⚜57

HOW MANY RATTLES? "That last puzzle made my head ache," said the White Queen. "Let's get back to arithmetic puzzles. Now, you know Tweedledum and Tweedledee?"

"Oh, yes, indeed!" replied Alice.

"Very well. Tweedledum and Tweedledee once had a wager."

"What was the wager about?" asked Alice.

"It was about the monstrous Crow. Tweedledum believed it would come back the next day, and Tweedledee believed it wouldn't. So they decided to have a wager about it."

"How much did they wager?" asked Alice.

"Well," replied the Queen, "you know they both collect rattles?"

"I know that Tweedledum had a rattle," replied Alice, "one that he claimed that Tweedledee had spoiled, but I didn't know that Tweedledee also had a rattle."

"They both had rattles," replied the Queen. "Indeed each had several rattles. The wager was for one rattle."

"How funny!" Alice laughed. "How many rattles did each have?"

"Ah, that is for you to figure out!" replied the Queen. "That is your problem. Now, Tweedledum realizes that if he loses the bet, then he will have the same number of rattles as Tweedledee, but if he wins the bet, then he will have twice as many rattles as Tweedledee. The question is, How many rattles does each one have?"

Now this problem is normally solved using algebra, but Alice knew no algebra. Fortunately, however, she remembered the lessons she had learned from the Gryphon, so she was able to get the answer. What is the answer?

### ♛ 58

HOW MANY BROTHERS AND SISTERS? "Here's another," said the Red Queen. "A little girl named Alice had a brother named Tony—"

"I don't have a brother named Tony," interrupted Alice.

"I wasn't talking about *you*," the Red Queen replied sharply. "I was talking about another Alice!"

"Oh!" replied Alice.

"And I wish you wouldn't keep interrupting!" continued the Queen. "Anyway, Alice and Tony had other brothers and sisters."

"Just a minute," interrupted Alice (not the Alice in the Looking-Glass, but the Alice at the party), "Tony and I don't have any other brothers or sisters!"

"The Red Queen wasn't talking about *you*," I replied, "but about still another Alice!"

"Oh!" replied Alice.

"Now," continued the Red Queen, "Tony has as many brothers as sisters. Alice has twice as many brothers as sisters. How many boys and how many girls are in the family?"

Alice solved this one.

### ♛ 59

HOW MANY WERE WRONG? "Here is one," said the White Queen, "and it happens to be a true story. I once had to post four letters. Well, I had the four letters written, and I had the four envelopes correctly addressed, but I was careless and put some of the letters into the wrong envelopes. However, I put only one letter in each envelope. As it happens, I either got exactly three of them right, or I got exactly two of them right, or I got exactly one of them wrong. How many did I get right?"

Alice got this one.

**♛ 60**

HOW MUCH LAND? "Let's see if you can do practical arithmetic," said the Red Queen. "A certain small farmer had no money to pay his taxes. As a result, the King's tax collector took one-tenth of his land away from him. After the land had been taken, the farmer had ten acres left. How much land did he originally have?"

Alice almost came out with the wrong answer, but checked herself just in time, thought a little more, and got it right. What is the answer?

**♛ 61**

ANOTHER ACREAGE PROBLEM "Here's another," said the Red Queen. "A different farmer had some farm land. On one-third of it

he cultivated squash, on one-fourth of it he cultivated peas, on one-fifth he cultivated beans, and on the remaining twenty-six acres he cultivated corn. How many acres did he have altogether?"

Alice got this one right. Can you? (No algebra is necessary!)

### ♛62

THE CLOCK STRIKES TWELVE "If a grandfather clock takes thirty seconds to strike six, how long does it take to strike twelve?" asked the Red Queen.

"Why, sixty seconds, of course!" exclaimed Alice. "Oh, no!" she suddenly realized, "that was wrong! Just a minute now, I'll tell you the correct answer!"

"Too late, too late!" exclaimed the Red Queen triumphantly. "Once you say something, you can never take it back!"

What is the correct answer?

### ♛63

THE TWELFTH QUESTION "Well, well, now," said the Red Queen, "you've already got three wrong, and we have only one question to go. Your passing or failing depends *entirely* on whether you get the next question right or wrong! Do you realize that?"

"Yes, I realize that," said Alice, a bit nervously.

"And being nervous won't help a bit!" added the Queen.

"I realize that, too," replied Alice, even more nervously.

"Now, child, here is the question—remember, *everything* depends on whether you answer it wrong or right!"

"Yes, yes, I know!" cried Alice.

"Well, the question is this: Will you pass this examination?"

"How should I know?" replied Alice, surprised at her own boldness.

"Tut, tut, child; that's no answer!" said the Red Queen. "You must give me a definite answer—yes or no. If you answer correctly, you will pass; if you don't you will fail—it's as simple as that!"

The matter didn't seem *quite* that simple to Alice! Indeed, the more she thought it over, the more puzzling it became. Then she suddenly realized something very interesting! If she answered one way, then the Red Queen would have the option of either passing her or failing her as she pleased. If she should answer the other way, then it would be impossible for the Queen either to pass her *or* fail her without contradicting her own rules! Well, since Alice was more interested in *not* failing than in passing, she chose the second alternative, and answered in such a way as totally to confound the Queen.

What answer did she give?

## CHAPTER 7

# *Tweedledum or Tweedledee?*

Alice's next adventure was far more pleasant. "I hate these examinations," said Alice to herself, shortly after she had left the company of the Queens. "They remind me so much of school!"

Just then Alice practically stumbled on Tweedledum and Tweedledee, who were grinning under a tree right by their house. Alice looked carefully at their collars to see which was marked "Dum" and which was marked "Dee," but neither collar was embroidered.

"I'm afraid I can't very well tell you apart without your embroidered collars," remarked Alice.

"You'll have to use *logic*," said one of the brothers, giving the other an affectionate hug. "We were expecting you to come around these parts, and we have prepared some nice logic games for you. Would you like to play?"

"What are the games?" asked Alice.

"Well, there are two games. The first is called Which of Us Is Tweedledee and Which Is Tweedledum? The second is called Which of Us Is Tweedledum and Which Is Tweedledee? Which game would you like to play first?"

"They sound so horribly alike," replied Alice. "It's dreadfully confusing!"

"Ah, they may *sound* alike," he replied, "but that doesn't mean they *are* alike, nohow!"

"Contrariwise," replied the other, "if they were alike, they wouldn't be, but if they weren't alike, they might be. Therefore, they're not alike. That's logic!"

It took Alice a bit of time to puzzle this out.

"If the names confuse you," said the first brother, "both games have alternative names. The first is also called Red and Black; and the second, Orange and Purple."

"What are the rules of the games?" asked Alice.

"Well, each game has six rounds," he replied. "Let us play the first game first—the game Red and Black."

At this point he pulled out a playing card from his pocket—it was the Queen of Diamonds—and showed it to Alice.

"As you see, this is a red card. Now, a red card signifies that the one carrying it is telling the truth, whereas a black card signifies that the speaker is telling a lie. Now, my brother there [he pointed to the other one] is also carrying either a red card or a black card in his pocket. He is about to make a statement. If his card is red, he will make a true statement, but if his card is black, he will make a false statement. Then your job is to figure out whether he is Tweedledee or Tweedledum."

"Oh, that sounds like fun!" said Alice. "I'd like to play!"

"After you have figured out who *he* is, your second job is to figure out who *I* am, you know!"

"Well, that part is just silly!" replied Alice, with a scream of laughter. "Obviously if he is Tweedledee, then you must be Tweedledum, and if he is Tweedledum, you must be Tweedledee. Even a dunce could figure *that* out!"

"Quite right," he replied, "and now let's play!"

*Game I—Red and Black*

♛64

ROUND ONE   At this point, the other brother said, "I am Tweedledum, and I am carrying a black card."

Alice had little difficulty in figuring out who he was. Who was he?

"Congratulations!" said both brothers at once, each shaking one of Alice's hands. "You have won the first round!"

"Now, for the next four rounds," said the first brother, "before each round, we both disappear into the house, where we have a pack of cards. We go into a huddle, then one of us puts a card in his pocket, comes out, and makes a statement. You must then figure out which one he is."

"Will he be carrying the same color card as in the last round?" asked Alice.

"Not necessarily" was the reply. "Each time we go into the house, the game begins afresh, and we are at liberty to change our cards or not."

"I understand," said Alice.

### ♛ 65

ROUND TWO   The brothers then went into the house, and, shortly after, one emerged with a card in his pocket and said, "If I am Tweedledum, then I am not carrying a red card."

Alice found this considerably more difficult than the first puzzle, but she finally managed to solve it. What is the solution?

### ♛ 66

ROUND THREE   In this round, a brother came out and said, "Either I am Tweedledum, or I am carrying a black card." Who was he?

### ♛ 67

ROUND FOUR   In this round, a brother came out and said, "Either I am Tweedledum carrying a black card, or I am Tweedledee carrying a red card."

Who was he?

### ♛ 68

ROUND FIVE   This time, the brother who emerged said, "Tweedledum is now carrying a black card."

Who was he?

"Very good!" he said to Alice. "You solved that one very nicely! Now, the last round of this game is more complicated: I go into the house, and my brother and I go into a huddle, and then *both* of us emerge, each with a red or a black card in his pocket. Our cards might be of the same color, or of different colors. Then we *both* make statements. You will have to take both statements into account to figure out who we are."

"That sounds more difficult!" said Alice.

"About twice as difficult," replied Tweedledee.

### ♛ 69

ROUND SIX  Well, Tweedledee went into the house, and both brothers came out shortly after.

They look more alike than ever! thought Alice.

Well, one of them—call him the first one—stood to Alice's left, and the other—call him the second one—stood to Alice's right. They then made the following statements:

> FIRST ONE: My brother is Tweedledee, and he is carrying a black card.
> SECOND ONE: My brother is Tweedledum, and he is carrying a red card.

Which one is which?

## Game II: Orange and Purple

"Congratulations!" cried both brothers. "You have won every round!"

"Now, the next game," said Tweedledum, "is much more interesting! It also has six rounds. Before each round, we go into the house where we have another pack of playing cards. These cards are colored orange and purple, rather than the usual red and black."

"Where did you ever get such cards?" asked Alice.

"We made them ourselves," he replied. "We made them specially for this occasion."

Alice thought it quite touching that they went to so much trouble for the sake of one occasion.

"Besides, they're very pretty cards, and they were fun to make," he added.

"Now," he continued, "one or both of us will come out of the house, and he (we) will make statements. Then you are to figure out who is who."

"Just a minute," said Alice, "you have not told me the significance of the colors orange and purple. Does one of them signify lying and the other truth-telling? And if so, which color means which?"

"Ah, that's the most interesting part of the game!" said Tweedledum. "You see, when *I* carry an orange card, it means that I am telling the truth, and when I carry a purple card, it means I am lying!"

"Contrariwise," said Tweedledee, "when *I* carry an orange card, it means I am lying, and when I carry a purple card, it means I am telling the truth!"

"Oh, that sounds *very* complicated!" remarked Alice.

"Not really," said Tweedledum, "not when you get used to it. Shall we try?"

"Ye-es," said Alice, a bit doubtfully.

ₘ 70

ROUND ONE    Both brothers went into the house. Shortly after, just one emerged and said, "My card is purple."

Alice had less trouble solving this than she had anticipated. Who was the speaker?

♛ 71

ROUND TWO  On the next round, both brothers came out and made the following statements:

FIRST ONE: I am Tweedledum.
SECOND ONE: I am Tweedledum.
FIRST ONE: My brother's card is orange.

Which one was Tweedledum?

♛ 72

ROUND THREE  On this round, the brothers made the following statements:

FIRST ONE: I am Tweedledee.
SECOND ONE: I am Tweedledum.
FIRST ONE: Our cards are of the same color.

Who is who?

♛ 73

ROUND FOUR  Alice found this round particularly interesting.

FIRST ONE: Our cards are both purple.
SECOND ONE: That is not true!

Who is who?

☞ 74

ROUND FIVE    This time the brothers made the following statements:

FIRST ONE: At least one of our cards is purple.
SECOND ONE: That is true.
FIRST ONE: I am Tweedledum.

Who is who?

☞ 75

ROUND SIX    "Now for this round," said one of the brothers, "the rules are the same, but the question you are to answer is different: Instead of telling us which one is Tweedledee and which one is Tweedledum, you are to figure out which one is lying and which one is telling the truth."

Both brothers went into the house, and when they came out, they made the following statements:

FIRST ONE: Our cards are of the same color.
SECOND ONE: Our cards are not of the same color.

Which one was telling the truth?

## Game III: Two Extra-Specials

Both brothers congratulated Alice warmly for having won every round.

"Before you leave," Tweedledee said with a grin, "we have two extra-specials for you! We will play two extra games, one round each, only the games will now be in sign language. We won't use colored cards this time. What we'll do is this: We will both go into the house, and one of us will come out first. The second one will come out soon after, carrying a large sign with a question written on it which both the first brother and you will be able to read clearly. Then the first brother will answer the question in sign language: He will draw either a square or a circle in the air. One of those two figures means yes and the other means no, but you will not be told which figure means what. However, the figure which *does* mean yes is already drawn on the *back* of the sign, but you will not be allowed to see it until after you have guessed which of us is Tweedledee and which is Tweedledum. The first brother (the one who answers the question) will, of course, have already seen the back of the sign, so he will know which of the square and circle means yes and which means no. However, he might lie when he gives his answer in sign language."

"I'm not sure I understand that," said Alice.

"Well, if, for example, the circle means yes, and the correct answer to the question is yes, then if he tells the truth, he will draw a circle in the air; if he lies, he will draw a square in the air."

"Oh, I understand!" said Alice.

"Good! Then we'll play the first game. One last thing: My brother and I have already agreed that if Tweedledee answers the question, he will lie, and if Tweedledum answers, he will tell the truth.

⬡76

WHO IS WHO? The brothers then went into the house. Almost immediately, one of them came out and stood in silence. Shortly

after, the other one came out bearing a sign, on the front of which
was written:

> IS THE FIGURE ON
> THE BACK OF THIS
> SIGN A SQUARE?

The other brother answered by drawing a circle in the air.
Which one was Tweedledum?

### ♛ 77

WHAT QUESTION SHOULD ALICE ASK? "Congratulations, you
did it again!" both brothers cried.

"Now comes the best game of all, and if you win it, you also win a
prize!" said Tweedledee.

"This time," he continued, "we have *not* agreed which of us lies
and which tells the truth. What we do is this: we go into the house,
and each one comes out, each with either a red or a black card in his
pocket. Again, red signifies truth-telling and black signifies lying.
Now, just one of us has a prize in his other pocket. If you can guess
which one of us has the prize, you get it. It now is not important
which of us is Tweedledee and which is Tweedledum; your job is to
find out which one has the prize. Now, when we come out of the
house, you point to one of us and ask him a question—a question
answerable by yes or no. But instead of answering yes or no, he will
again answer in sign language: He will draw either a square or a
circle in the air. Now, the important point is this: if he is carrying
the prize, then by a square he means yes and by a circle he means
no. On the other hand, if he is not the one who is carrying the prize,
then by a square he means no and by a circle he means yes. On top
of that, he might tell the truth or he might lie—this is determined
by whether he is carrying a red card or a black card."

"But what question am I supposed to ask him?" inquired Alice.

"Ah, that is for *you* to figure out!" he triumphantly replied.
"That's the hardest part of the game, and if you can figure out the
right question, you certainly *deserve* a prize."

"Well," said Alice, "I'm afraid I can't do this without pencil and paper, and I forgot to bring my memorandum book in this journey into the Looking-Glass."

Tweedledee quickly went into the house and returned with a pencil and a pad of paper.

"We'll be in the house while you are figuring out your question, and when you are ready, call us and we will come out. Take as much time as you like."

The brothers then went into the house, and Alice worked quite hard on the puzzle. After a while, she shouted, "I'm ready." The brothers then came out, Alice asked one of them a question, and he replied by drawing either a square or a circle in the air. Alice pointed to one of the two brothers and said, "You're the one who is carrying the prize," and Alice was right.

How, in one question, could Alice find out which one has the prize?

"Congratulations again!" said both brothers. "You have certainly earned your prize!"

Alice was then given her prize, all nicely wrapped and tied together. The more she tried unwrapping it, the tighter it got!

"Have you forgotten that you're in the Looking-Glass?" asked one of the brothers.

"Oh, of course!" remembered Alice, who then tried *wrapping* it and making the string tighter. This worked like magic; the parcel almost immediately unwrapped itself.

The prize consisted of a pencil and a beautiful brand-new memorandum book.

## CHAPTER 8

# *And That's the Beautiful Part of It!*

"That was really fun!" said Alice to herself, shortly after she had left the Tweedle brothers. "It's so much better than taking those nasty old examinations! And I *love* this memorandum book—just what I needed!'"

At this point Alice sat down on a ledge and spent quite some time jotting down the various adventures she wished to remember—particularly the logic games she had just been playing with Tweedledum and Tweedledee. She filled the first nine pages of her book.

And now, thought Alice, rising, I must be getting on. I wonder if I'll meet the White Knight? I'd love to see him—I have so much to tell him!

Shortly after, Alice came upon Humpty Dumpty sitting on the very same spot of the same wall. When he saw her, he grinned from ear to ear.

"Nice work, nice work!" he said.

"What was nice work?" asked Alice.

"Why, the way you fooled those Queens with that twelfth question! Serves them both right! Serves them right for giving you that fool examination!"

"Oh, you know about it?" asked Alice.

"Now, if *I* were to give you an examination," began Humpty Dumpty.

"Oh, you needn't!" said Alice hastily.

"If I were to give you an examination," repeated Humpty Dumpty, "what do you think I would do?"

"I'm sure I haven't the slightest idea!" replied Alice, a bit anxiously.

"Why, child, if I were to give you an examination—not that I would, you know—but *if* I were to give you an examination, then I would ask you only questions which have no answers; they are the best kind, you know!"

"What's the sense of a question without an answer?" asked Alice.

"Ah, that's the kind that makes you *think!*" he replied.

"Think about *what?*" asked Alice.

"About what the answer could be," he replied.

"But I thought you said there was no answer."

"There isn't," replied Humpty Dumpty, "and that's the beautiful part of it!"

Alice tried to puzzle this out. It didn't quite seem to make sense.

"Can you give me an example of such a question?" asked Alice.

"Ah, now you talk like a sensible child!" replied Humpty Dumpty. "Surely I can give you an example. Indeed, I can think offhand of two examples. Which one would you like me to give you first?"

"How could I know?" asked Alice. "Since I have no idea what examples you have in mind, how could I possibly tell you which one to give me?"

"Right again," replied Humpty. "That's what I call being a logical child! Well, then, here's a perfect example of the kind of question I have in mind. The question is this: Is No the correct answer to this question?"

"To what question?" asked Alice.

"Why, to the question I just asked!" replied Humpty Dumpty.

Alice thought about this for a moment. "No," she answered, "of course not!"

"Ah, I've caught you!" exclaimed Humpty Dumpty proudly.

"How so?" asked Alice.

"Look, child, you answered no, did you not?"

"Of course I did!" replied Alice.

"And did you answer correctly?" asked Humpty Dumpty.

"Certainly," replied Alice, "why not?"

"Ah, that's where I have you!" he replied. "Since you answered no and you answered correctly, then no *is* the correct answer to the question!"

"That's what I'm saying!" said Alice.

"Well, if No is the correct answer, then when I asked you whether it was, you should have said yes, not no!"

Alice thought about this for a while and suddenly saw the point. "Of course!" said Alice. "You're absolutely right! I should have said yes, not no!"

"Ah, I've caught you again!" replied Humpty Dumpty triumphantly.

"What!" said Alice in amazement.

"Of course I have, child! Yes can't possibly be the right answer!"

"Why not?" asked Alice, more puzzled than ever.

"To answer yes is to affirm that No is the correct answer, but if no is the correct answer, you should give *it* rather than the incorrect answer Yes!"

"Oh!" said Alice, more bewildered than ever. "So I guess I was right the first time; I should have answered no after all."

"No, you *shouldn't* have," said Humpty Dumpty sharply. "I've already proven that!"

"I give up!" said Alice wearily. "What is the correct answer?"

"Why, there *is* no correct answer," he replied in a tone of complete triumph, "and that's the beautiful part of it!"

"Where did you ever get that baffling question?" asked Alice.

"I thought it up myself!" replied Humpty Dumpty proudly. "And wasn't I right?"

"Right about what?" asked Alice.

"Didn't the question make you *think*?"

"It certainly did!" replied Alice. "It almost made my head ache! Is this question an example of what is called a paradox?"

"Indeed it is, child, and a fine one at that! I thought it up myself."

"I know that," said Alice. "You've already repeated it twice."

"Not so," replied Humpty Dumpty, "I've *said* it twice, but I *repeated* it only once.

"Anyhow," he continued, "paradoxes are usually in the form of statements rather than questions. Mine is novel in that it is in the form of a question rather than a statement. It is based on the idea behind the famous statement which asserts its own falsehood."

"What statement is that?" asked Alice.

"It is the following well-known statement—here, let me write it for you."

Alice handed him her pencil and memorandum book. Humpty Dumpty glanced through the first nine pages.

"This is interesting stuff," he said, "but you've forgotten to number the pages. You should always number the pages, you know! Otherwise, how can you tell which page follows which?"

"But the pages are not *loose*," replied Alice. "They are bound together. So it is obvious which page follows which!"

"You should always number your pages," repeated Humpty Dumpty. "Here—I'll number them for you."

He then numbered the first nine pages, then the tenth and

eleventh pages, which were still blank. Then he wrote the following on the tenth page and handed it back to Alice.

> —10—
>
> THE SENTENCE
> ON PAGE 10
> IS FALSE.

"Now," said Humpty Dumpty, "is the statement on page ten of your book true or false?"

"I see no way to tell," replied Alice, after thinking it over for a bit. "It could be either."

"Wrong!" exclaimed Humpty Dumpty. "It's not that it *could* be either—it's that it *couldn't* be either!"

"Why not?" asked Alice.

"Now look, child; could the sentence possibly be true?"

"Why not?" asked Alice.

"Well, suppose it were true. Then what it says must be the case. But what it *says* is that it is false. Therefore, it must be the case that it is false. So if it is true, it is also false. But it is impossible that it can be both true and false; therefore it is impossible that it is true."

"Of course," said Alice, "and since it cannot possibly be true, then it must be false."

"Wrong again!" said Humpty Dumpty triumphantly. "It can't be false either!"

"Why not?" asked Alice.

"Well, suppose it *were* false. Then what it says is *not* the case. Now, what it says is that it is false. Since what it says is *not* the case, then it is not the case that it is false—in other words, it is true. So if it is false, then it is true, and we again have a contradiction. Therefore, it can't be false. That's glory for you!"

"Oh, dear," said Alice disconsolately. "I seem to be in the same predicament as with your first puzzle!"

"Exactly!" replied Humpty Dumpty, "and that's the beautiful part of it!"

"Actually," said Alice, "I heard something like that paradox before: It is the story of Epimenides the Cretan, who said, 'All Cretans are liars.' If Epimenides is telling the truth, then he is lying, and if he is lying, then he is telling the truth. So we have a paradox."

"Not true!" said Humpty Dumpty, decisively. "That is a popular fallacy! This is one of these things which *seems* like a paradox, but really isn't one."

"Will you please explain?" asked Alice.

"In the first place, what do you mean by a liar?—one who lies all the time, or one who lies some of the time?"

"I had never thought of that before," admitted Alice. "I guess one who lies even some of the time should be called a liar."

"Then there is *certainly* no paradox," replied Humpty Dumpty. "Epimenides' statement could be true, which would then mean only that all Cretans *sometimes* lie. Then Epimenides, being a Cretan, also sometimes lies, but that does not mean that the particular statement in question is a lie. Thus there is no paradox."

"I see," said Alice. "Then I guess I had better define a liar as one who *always* lies. Then we get a paradox?"

"No, even then we don't," replied Humpty Dumpty. "This time we do know that Epimenides' statement can't be true, because if it were, then all Cretans would always lie, and Epimenides, being a Cretan, would always lie, hence would have lied when he made that statement. So if the statement were true, it would also have to be false, which is a contradiction."

"Then it *is* a paradox!" said Alice.

"No! No!" said Humpty Dumpty. "A contradiction only arises if we assume the statement true; if the statement is false, there is no contradiction!"

"Will you please explain that?" asked Alice.

"Well, what does it mean for the statement to be false? It means that it is not the case that all Cretans are liars—in other words, that at least one Cretan sometimes tells the truth. So all that emerges from Epimenides' having made the statement is that he is lying and that at least one Cretan sometimes tells the truth. This is no paradox!"

"That's interesting!" said Alice.

"Incidentally," added Humpty Dumpty, "if we made the additional two assumptions that Epimenides is the *only* Cretan, and that the statement he made is the only statement he ever made in his life, then we would have a paradox! It would then be just like the statement I wrote down in your book which asserts its own falsehood."

"Come to think of it," added Humpty Dumpty, "I'd like to try another experiment. May I have your memorandum book again?"

Alice handed him the book with a pencil. Humpty Dumpty wrote something, handed the book back, and said, "Look on page eleven. Is the statement there true or false?"

Alice turned to page 11, and here is what she found:

```
┌──────────────────┐
│      —11—         │
│                   │
│  THE SENTENCE     │
│  ON PAGE 11       │
│  IS TRUE.         │
└──────────────────┘
```

Alice thought about this for a while.

"I see no way to tell," replied Alice. "It seems to me that it could be either: If it were true, there would be no contradiction; and if it were false, there also wouldn't be any contradiction."

"This time you're absolutely right!" said Humpty Dumpty. "Now, that's what I call being chameleonic!"

"What *ever* did you mean by that?" asked Alice in astonishment.

"All I meant is that sometimes you are wrong and sometimes you are right—just like a chameleon is sometimes one color and sometimes another."

This seemed to Alice a most odd use of the word chameleonic—still (as Alice recalled) Humpty Dumpty sometimes has his own very special way of using words!

"Now, I'd like to try something else," said Humpty Dumpty. "Let me have your notebook again."

Humpty Dumpty took it and on pages 10, 11 he erased the

figures 10 and 11 in both sentences and rewrote 11, 10 in their places, so the pages now looked like this:

| —10— | —11— |
|------|------|
| THE SENTENCE ON PAGE 11 IS FALSE. | THE SENTENCE ON PAGE 10 IS TRUE. |

"Now," said Humpty Dumpty, "is the sentence on page eleven true or false?"

Alice thought about this for some time and suddenly saw the solution.

"It couldn't be either," she said. "It's again a paradox!"

"Right you are!" said Humpty Dumpty. "Only how would you prove it?"

"Well," said Alice, "the sentence on page eleven is really asserting its own falsehood—only indirectly: it affirms the sentence on page ten which asserts the falsehood of the sentence on page eleven. So if the sentence on page eleven is true, it must also be false, and if it is false, it must also be true. So we have a paradox."

"Now you're really learning!" exclaimed Humpty Dumpty in a satisfied tone.

"Actually there is one paradox I could *never* figure out!" said Alice. "Perhaps you can help me?"

"Indeed, I'll be glad to," said Humpty Dumpty proudly. "I can solve any puzzle that's ever been invented, and a lot more that haven't. What's your problem?"

"It's the one about the barber," replied Alice. "A certain barber living in a small town shaves all the inhabitants who don't shave themselves and never shaves any inhabitant who does shave himself. Does the barber shave himself or not?"

"Oh, that's an old one, and a very easy one!" laughed Humpty Dumpty.

"I can't see any possible solution!" said Alice. "I've thought it over and can't get anywhere! If the barber shaves himself, then he is violating his rule by shaving someone who shaves himself. If he doesn't shave himself, then he is one of those who don't shave themselves, and since he shaves all such people, then he must shave himself. So whether he shaves himself or not, you get a contradiction! Now, you can't get out of this one by saying, 'It's neither true nor false that he shaves himself,' because it *must* be either true or false that he shaves himself!"

"That *who* shaves himself?" asked Humpty Dumpty.

"Why the barber, of course!"

"Which barber?" asked Humpty Dumpty.

"Obviously the barber of the story!" replied Alice, a bit impatiently.

"Oh, really now?" said Humpty, "and who ever said the story is true?"

Alice thought about this for a moment.

"Come now," said Alice, "it is *given* that the barber is as described; in approaching a puzzle, one can't deny what's given!"

"Can't one?" replied Humpty Dumpty, "even when the so-called given is self-contradictory?"

This was a new idea to Alice.

"The fact is," continued Humpty Dumpty, "there *is* no such barber, there never has been any such barber, and there never *will* be any such barber. There simply *couldn't* be such a barber, because if there were, you would have a contradiction."

Alice was not quite convinced.

"Now look," said Humpty Dumpty, a bit irritatedly, "suppose I told you that there was a man, and he was six feet tall, and he wasn't six feet tall—what would you say?"

"Obviously that there was no such man," replied Alice.

"Good! And suppose I told you that there was a barber who neither shaved himself nor didn't shave himself—what would you say?"

"That there was no such barber," replied Alice.

"Well, that's exactly the barber of this story! Such a barber could neither shave himself nor not shave himself. Ergo, there is no such barber. That's logic for you!"

This completely convinced Alice.

"There is a related problem which will put this problem in a still better light," continued Humpty Dumpty. "In a certain town there are *two* barbers—call them Barber A and Barber B. It is given that Barber A shaves all the inhabitants who don't shave themselves, but it is *not* given that he doesn't shave some other inhabitants as well. As for Barber B, he never shaves any inhabitant who shaves himself, but he doesn't necessarily shave *all* inhabitants who don't shave themselves. Now, it is perfectly possible that Barbers A and B exist; there is no contradiction in assuming they do."

"Then what's the problem?" asked Alice.

"The problem has two parts: Does Barber A shave himself or doesn't he? And does Barber B shave himself or doesn't he?"

Alice thought about this for a bit. "Barber A shaves himself and Barber B doesn't," answered Alice, quite proudly.

"Good! Very good!" Humpty Dumpty exclaimed. "Now, can you tell me why?"

"Because," replied Alice, quite confidently, "if Barber A didn't shave himself, then he would be one of those who don't shave themselves, but since he shaves all such people, he would have to shave himself. This is a contradiction. Therefore, he doesn't shave himself. As for Barber B, if he shaves himself, then he would be shaving someone who shaves himself, which he never does. Therefore, Barber B can't shave himself."

"Now you're learning!" said Humpty Dumpty. "It's really lucky for you that you have such a good teacher!"

Alice did not quite know what to say to this; Humpty Dumpty's logic sessions were certainly most instructive. Yet, she thought, he does seem to be a *little* on the boastful side!

"You said this puts the old barber puzzle in a new light," said Alice. "What is the relationship between the two puzzles?"

"Oh, I'm glad you asked that," he replied. "Well, you see, there could be a barber like Barber A, and such a barber must shave himself. Also there could be a barber like Barber B, only such a barber could not shave himself. However, you can't have Barber A and Barber B being the same person! Now, in the original problem, you were given *one* person who had both the properties of Barber A and of Barber B, and *that* is impossible!"

"Oh, I see!" said Alice, "that is interesting!"

"Here's another puzzle for you," said Humpty Dumpty, "and this one does have a definite answer. You know the one about the Hearts Club?"

"No," replied Alice, "I've never heard that one before."

"Good," he replied, "you got that one right!"

"I got *what* right?" asked Alice.

"The question I asked you! I asked you whether you know the puzzle about the Hearts Club, and you said you never heard it before, and you were right!"

"Well, yes," said Alice, "of course I was right, only how could you have known it?"

"Because I invented the puzzle myself, and I've never told it to anyone before, so you *must* have been right!"

"Oh!" said Alice. "But what is the puzzle of the Hearts Club?"

"Well," he replied, "in a certain community, the inhabitants have formed various clubs. One particular club is called the Hearts Club. We are given the following facts:

"(One) Given any lady in the community, if she does not belong to every club, then she belongs to the Hearts Club.

"(Two) No man can be a member of the Hearts Club unless there is at least one other club of which he is not a member.

"(Three) Given any club, every man outside the club loves every lady in the Hearts Club.

96

"Now," continued Humpty Dumpty, "Lillian is a lady of the community, but it is not given whether or not she is a member of the Hearts Club. Richard is a man of the community, and it is also not given whether or not he is a member of the Hearts Club. Can it be determined whether or not Richard loves Lillian?"

"I don't see how!" replied Alice.

"Ah, that's because you don't think!" replied Humpty Dumpty. "Yes, child," he continued, "it is possible to determine it. In fact— ah, you may not believe what I am going to tell you! What I am going to tell you—oh, yes, you may well look surprised! What I am going to tell you is that in such a town, *all* the men must love *all* the ladies!"

Alice thought about this. "I still don't see why," she finally said.

"Well, child, it follows from the first premise that every lady in the town must belong to the Hearts Club. Why? Because, take any lady: either she doesn't belong to all clubs or she does belong to all clubs. If the former, then, by the first premise, she must belong to the Hearts Club. If the latter, then of course she belongs to the Hearts Club, since the Hearts Club is one of all the clubs. So in either case, she belongs to the Hearts Club. This proves that all the ladies in town belong to the Hearts Club."

"I see that," said Alice.

"Well," continued Humpty Dumpty, "it follows from the second

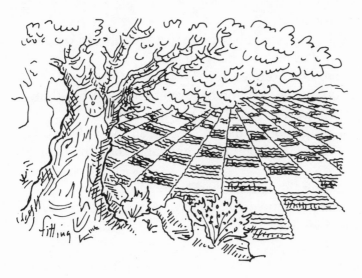

premiss that no man in the town belongs to all the clubs. Why? Because if a man belonged to all the clubs, then he would belong to the Hearts Club in particular, yet no man belonging to all the clubs can belong to the Hearts Club. Therefore, no man belongs to all the clubs."

"I see that," said Alice.

"This means," he continued, "that every man is outside at least one club, but any man outside any club loves all the ladies in the Hearts Club. Therefore, all the men in town love all the ladies in the Hearts Club, but since all the ladies are in the Hearts Club, then all the men in town love all the ladies in town."

"That was interesting!" said Alice. "Tell me another!"

"Well," said Humpty Dumpty, "would you believe it if I told you I had a baby?"

"Why not?" said Alice.

"And would you also believe it if I told you that everybody loves my baby?"

"Why not?" said Alice.

"And would you also believe it if I told you that my baby loves only me?"

"I don't see why not," replied Alice.

"Ah!" said Humpty Dumpty, "if you believed *all* those things, then you'd be inconsistent!"

"Why?" asked Alice.

"Or at least you would be driven to a very absurd conclusion: You don't believe I'm my own baby, do you?"

"Of course not!" replied Alice.

"Well, you'd *have* to if you believed all those other things!"

"Why?" asked Alice, who was very puzzled.

"It's just simple logic, that's all. Look, suppose those other things were true. Since everyone loves my baby, then my baby also loves my baby."

"Oh, I hadn't thought of that!" said Alice.

"Of course not, but you *should* have, you know. You should always think of everything."

"I can't think of *everything!*" replied Alice.

"I never said you *could*," replied Humpty Dumpty. "I merely said you *should*."

"But is it reasonable to say that I should do something that I cannot do?" asked Alice.

"That is an interesting problem in Moral Philosophy," he replied, "but that would take us too far afield. Coming back to this problem, since my baby loves himself and also loves *only* me, it would follow that I am my own baby! Therefore, not everything I told you can be true."

"That was a funny one!" said Alice.

"True," replied Humpty Dumpty, "and now I would like to tell you a rather special puzzle. It's one I invented myself, but I'm not sure I know the answer to it! It seems like a paradox, but I'm not absolutely sure it is."

Alice was very curious as to what sort of puzzle could possibly confound Humpty Dumpty himself!

"Well, it's like this," he began. "You know puzzles about knights who always tell the truth and knaves who always lie?"

"Oh, many indeed!" replied Alice.

"Well, then, suppose you are in a land inhabited entirely by knights who always tell the truth and knaves who always lie. You meet one inhabitant about whom you know nothing—all you know is that he is either a knight or a knave, but you have no idea which. He makes but one statement: *You do not and never will know that I am a knight.* What would you conclude?"

"Well, let's see," said Alice. "Suppose he is a knave. Then his statement is false, which means that I do or will know that he's a knight. But if I *know* that he is a knight, then he must in fact be one (because whatever is known must be true). Therefore, if he is a knave, then he must be a knight, which is a contradiction. So he can't be a knave; so he must be a knight."

"Then you know he is a knight," said Humpty Dumpty.

"Yes," said Alice, "but that makes further trouble! Since I know he is a knight, then his statement that I do not and never will know that he is a knight—this statement must be false, which makes him a knave! So we have a paradox."

"So it seems," said Humpty Dumpty, "and yet—"

"I guess the only solution is that the given conditions are impossible," interrupted Alice. "No inhabitant of a knight-knave land could ever make such a statement."

"So it would seem," replied Humpty Dumpty, "and yet—"

Here Humpty Dumpty paused and got lost deeply in thought.

"And yet, *what?*" asked Alice.

"And yet, child, I don't really know—I say a knight *could* have made that statement—at least to *you* he could."

"Why to *me?*" asked Alice.

"Because of the way you reacted!" replied Humpty Dumpty. "Suppose you actually went to such a land and met an inhabitant who *did* make that statement. What would you make of it?"

"I told you," replied Alice, "that I would be doubtful that the given conditions applied. In other words, I would be doubtful that the knights always told the truth and the knaves always lied."

"Then you would have no idea whether the speaker was a knight or a knave?"

"Of course not," replied Alice, "how could I?"

"Then the fellow told the truth after all, so he could be a knight and it could be that the given conditions *do* hold!"

"Oh, dear," said Alice, "it seems that whatever I say is wrong!"

"Exactly!" replied Humpty Dumpty triumphantly. "And that's the beautiful part of it!"

## CHAPTER 9

# The White Knight Couldn't Quite Remember

"Humpty Dumpty is really one of the most confusing characters I've ever met!" thought Alice, sometime after she had left him seated in deep thought upon the wall. "And at the same time," she continued to herself, "he is so remarkably logical! I wonder how he manages to be both confusing *and* logical?"

Just then Alice spied her old friend the White Knight way off in the distance, slowly riding in her direction. Of all Alice's puzzle-adventures in the Looking-Glass, those that now follow are the ones she remembered most vividly. For years after, she kept telling her friends these fascinating and unusual puzzles.

The White Knight saw Alice from the distance, waved, and promptly tumbled off his horse.

"Oh, dear!" thought Alice. "There he goes again! Maybe he really should have a wooden horse with wheels after all!"

Well, the Knight was not the least bit hurt (having fallen headlong into his sugar-loaf helmet); he remounted and, after about five or six more tumbles, finally reached Alice. He was delighted to see her and to hear all about her latest adventures. He was particularly interested in the trials in Wonderland concerning the stolen tarts.

"As to trials," said the White Knight, "I've been to some of the finest trials in the world!"

"Oh, please tell me some!" said Alice, who was very interested in these matters.

"Oh, yes," said the White Knight, "they were very fine, very fine!"

"But will you *tell* me some?" asked Alice.

"Very fine trials," repeated the Knight. "Why only last week—or maybe it was the week before last—I attended a trial."

"What was the trial about?" asked Alice.

"Well, I don't quite remember exactly what the trial was *about,* but I remember it was about something or other."

"I would imagine so," replied Alice, who could hardly refrain from laughing. "It isn't usual to have a trial about nothing!"

"Quite right, quite right," replied the Knight. "The trial was *definitely* about something; the only trouble is that I can't quite remember just what that something was! It seems that someone or other had done something he wasn't supposed to have done, and so there was a trial."

There was a long pause.

"Do you remember anything else?" asked Alice.

"I remember that there were three defendants and that just one of them was guilty."

"Oh, good," replied Alice. "Who were the defendants?"

"Who were the defendants?" repeated the White Knight. "Who were they? I can't quite remember just *who* they were, but I definitely remember there were three of them."

"Well, what happened at the trial?" asked Alice.

"What happened?" repeated the Knight. "Why, the defendants made statements!"

"What statements did they make?" asked Alice, who was getting just a *little* impatient with the rather slow way the account was going.

"What statements?" repeated the Knight. "What statements? I can't quite remember just *what* the statements were, but I do remember that they made statements."

"Really now!" said Alice, who was getting quite exasperated. "Don't you remember *anything* about the statements?"

"Oh, yes," replied the White Knight, "I remember *something* about them. The first defendant accused either the second defendant or the third defendant, but I don't remember which one."

"What about the second defendant?" asked Alice.

"Well, the second defendant was asked who was guilty, and to everyone's surprise he claimed to be the guilty one."

"And the third defendant?" asked Alice.

"Well, the third defendant was asked who was guilty, and either he accused himself or he accused the second defendant, but unfortunately I can't quite remember which."

Alice tried to puzzle all this out, but could not make head or tail of what went on.

"Tell me," said Alice, "did the innocent defendants both know who the guilty defendant was?"

"Oh, yes," replied the Knight, "the defendants all knew who was guilty."

"Then I guess some of the defendants lied, and maybe some told the truth. Is that it?"

"That's right," replied the Knight. "Some of them lied and some of them told the truth."

"Can you remember which ones lied and which ones told the truth?" asked Alice.

"Well," replied the White Knight, "I remember that the guilty one lied. As for the innocent ones, I remember that either one of them told the truth, or maybe the other one did, or maybe they both did, but I can't remember which."

This concluded the White Knight's account. Of all the trial accounts I have ever heard in my life, thought Alice, this is the most unsatisfactory! Yet, as Alice pondered more and more over this problem, she came to realize that despite all the White Knight's memory lapses, he had given her enough information to decide whether the first, the second, or the third defendant was guilty.

Which one was guilty? (This is Problem ♛78.)

### ♛79

THE SECOND ACCOUNT "Yes, I've seen some fine trials, some very fine ones!" said the Knight, after Alice had solved the last puzzle.

"Tell me another," requested Alice.

The puzzle which now follows is one of the best that Alice had ever heard.

"Well," said the Knight, "the trial of last month was quite interesting. Again there were three defendants, and only one of them was guilty. The first defendant spoke first, then the second defendant spoke, and the third defendant spoke last."

"But what did they *say*?" asked Alice.

"I don't quite remember what they *said*," replied the Knight, "but I do remember that each of the defendants accused one of the others. However, I can't remember who accused whom. And now, can you figure out who was guilty?"

"Of course not!" replied Alice. "So far you have told me practically nothing! Could you at least tell me which ones lied and which ones told the truth?"

"Very interesting that you should have asked that," replied the Knight, "because two weeks ago I told this case to the White King, who had been unable to attend the trial. The White King asked me the very same question, and when I told him which of the three lied and which ones told the truth, he was able to deduce who the guilty one was."

"Oh, good!" said Alice. "Which ones did lie and which ones did tell the truth?"

"Alas, I have forgotten that by now!" replied the Knight.

"Then I guess it's hopeless for me to solve the mystery," said Alice sadly.

"That's very remarkable that you should have said that!" replied the Knight. "Because the same thing happened to me last week. I met Humpty Dumpty and told the case to him. I also told him that I had told the White King about the case a week earlier and that the White King was able to solve it after I told him which ones lied and which ones told the truth. Then Humpty Dumpty asked me which ones had lied and which ones had told the truth, but by then I had forgotten, so I couldn't answer Humpty Dumpty's question. Then Humpty Dumpty also said, 'Then I guess it is hopeless for me to solve it.'"

"So Humpty Dumpty didn't solve it," said Alice.

"Oh, yes, he did, because he asked me another question, and when I answered, he was able to solve it."

"What question was that?" asked Alice eagerly.

"Unfortunately I have forgotten by now," replied the White Knight.

"It is very difficult to get information from you," said Alice. "Don't you remember *anything* about the question?"

"Yes," replied the Knight, "I remember that Humpty Dumpty either asked me whether any two consecutive statements were true, or he asked me whether any two consecutive statements were false, but I can't remember which of the two questions he asked, or what answer I gave."

Which of the three defendants was guilty?

### ♛ 80

THE NEXT TRIAL "I remember another curious trial," said the White Knight. "It involved three defendants. Each of the three accused one of the other two. The first defendant was the only one who told the truth. Had each one accused someone different, but again not himself, then the second defendant would have been the only one who told the truth."

Which of the three defendants was guilty?

### ♛ 81

THE NEXT TRIAL "Another trial I know about," said the White Knight, "is one in which I was not present. It was told to me by the Jabberwocky.

"As the Jabberwocky explained, there were again three defendants. Each of them accused one of the others, but the Jabberwocky didn't tell me who accused whom. However, he did tell me that the first defendant told the truth."

"What about the second defendant?" asked Alice.

"The Jabberwocky never told me whether the second defendant told the truth or lied."

"And the third?" asked Alice.

"The Jabberwocky told me whether the third defendant had lied or told the truth, but unfortunately I cannot now remember what he told me. All I do remember is that at the time the Jabberwocky told me, I was able to determine which of the three defendants was guilty, but now I've forgotten which one it was."

Which of the three defendants was guilty?

♛82

ANOTHER CASE "I remember being told about a rather similar trial," continued the Knight. "Again there were three defendants; each accused one of the others, and the first one told the truth. Again the Jabberwocky didn't tell me whether the second lied or told the truth, but he did tell me whether the third lied or told the truth. This information was not enough to enable me to deduce who was guilty. Then the Jabberwocky told me who the third defendant accused, and I could then determine who was guilty. But I no longer remember whether the third one lied or told the truth, nor do I remember whom he accused."

Who was guilty this time?

## ♛ 83

ANOTHER CASE "There was one trial at which I was present and the Jabberwocky absent," said the White Knight. "Again there were three defendants, and only one was guilty. The first defendant was asked whether he was guilty, and he answered yes or no, but I can't remember which. Then the second defendant was asked whether he was guilty, and he answered yes or no, but again I can't remember which. Then the third defendant was asked whether the first defendant was innocent or guilty, and he either said the first defendant was innocent, or he said the first defendant was guilty, but I no longer remember which it was. Do you have any idea yet who was guilty?"

"Of course not!" replied Alice.

"I figured not," said the Knight. "However, I also remember something else: I don't remember which ones told the truth and which ones lied, but I do remember that at least one of them told the truth and at least one of them lied. Now can you figure out who was guilty?"

"Surely not!" replied Alice.

"I figured not," said the White Knight, "but if it will help you any, let me tell you that last week I met the Jabberwocky, who asked me about the trial. At that time I still remembered what each defendant had said, and I told the Jabberwocky what each one had said. I also told the Jabberwocky that at least one of the three statements was true and that at least one was false. The Jabberwocky was then able to figure out who was guilty."

At this point Alice—and also you—have enough information to solve the case.

Who was guilty?

♛84

ANOTHER CASE "I remember another trial at which I was present," began the White Knight. "Again there were three defendants, and only one of them was guilty. I remember that the first defendant accused the second defendant, but I can't at all remember what either the second or third defendant said. I also remember that last week I told the case to the Red Queen, and I told her another fact which I cannot now quite remember. I either told her that the guilty one was the only one who lied, or I told her that the guilty one was the only one who told the truth, but I can't remember which. But I do remember that the Red Queen was able to solve the case."

Who was guilty?

♛85

AND THIS CASE? "There was one trial about which I remember a great deal," said the White Knight. "I remember that there were again three defendants and that only one of them was guilty. I distinctly remember that the first defendant accused the second defendant, and the second defendant accused himself. Then the third defendant either accused himself, or he accused the first defendant, but I can't remember which.

"I told this problem to Humpty Dumpty some time ago," continued the White Knight, "and Humpty Dumpty asked me how many of the three statements were true. I can't remember now what I told him, but after I told him, Humpty Dumpty was able to solve the case."

Who was guilty?

♛86

WHAT WAS THE FATE OF THE GOAT? "Yes, I've seen some fine trials, very fine, very fine!" continued the White Knight. "I remember one curious one, and I even remember who the defendants were!"

"That's refreshing!" said Alice.

"Oh, yes, it was a very fine trial! The three defendants were the Goat, the Beetle, and the Gnat."

"I remember them well," said Alice, recalling her adventures with the Looking-Glass Insects.

"The Goat was the main suspect," continued the Knight. "First the Goat accused one of the insects—either he accused the Beetle or he accused the Gnat—but I can't quite remember which. Then the Beetle either accused the Gnat or he accused the Goat, but I can't remember which one. Then the Gnat accused one of the other two, but unfortunately I no longer remember which one he accused."

Oh, dear, thought Alice, I'm going to have trouble again!

"I also remember," continued the Knight, "that other evidence came up, and the Court either knew that the Goat lied, or they knew that both insects told the truth, but I can't remember which—maybe it was both."

"Was the Goat convicted or not?" asked Alice.

"I don't quite remember what *did* happen," replied the Knight, "but I do remember that either the Court convicted the Goat, or they acquitted the Goat, or they did neither."

"Well, of course the Court did one of those three things!" cried

Alice. "One doesn't have to *remember* that; it's a simple matter of logic!"

"Quite right," said the Knight, "and yet I seem to remember it so vividly!"

"Anything else you remember?" asked Alice.

"Well, a few days ago I met the Gentleman dressed in white paper—the one you once met on the train. He was unable to attend this trial, but he was quite interested in what happened, since he personally knew each of the three defendants. I told him all I have told you so far, and, in addition, I remembered at the time whether it was that the Goat had lied or whether it was that the two Insects had told the truth. When I told him which, he was able to determine whether the Goat was convicted, acquitted, or whether the Court was undecided."

Was the Goat convicted, acquitted, or was the Court undecided?

### ♛ 87

THE MOST BAFFLING CASE OF ALL   Of all the trials that the White Knight recounted, the one that follows is the one that remained most firmly in Alice's memory. At first it seemed so utterly impossible to solve, and yet, with further reflection, it completely succumbed to logical analysis.

"In this trial," began the White Knight, "there were again three defendants, and only one was guilty. The first defendant either claimed that he was innocent, or he claimed he was guilty, but I can't remember which. Then the second defendant either claimed that he was innocent, or he claimed to be guilty, but again I can't remember which. Then the third defendant either accused the first defendant, or he claimed that the first defendant was innocent, but again I cannot remember which. However, I vividly remember that *at most* one of the three statements was true.

"Last month," continued the Knight, "I met the Jabberwocky and I told him all I have told you so far. Also, at that time, I remembered what each of the three defendants said, and when I told the Jabberwocky what each had said, he was able to solve the case."

"I see," said Alice, "and now, given this additional information about the Jabberwocky, *I* should be able to solve the case. Is that it?"

"No," replied the White Knight thoughtfully, "no, no, you don't have enough information yet."

"What else do I need to know?"

"Well," replied the Knight, "a week after I spoke to the Jabberwocky, I met Tweedledee, who takes an interest in these matters, and told him everything I have told you so far. Of course, he could not solve the case any more than you can now do. However, he asked me if I could remember what the first defendant had said. Fortunately, I could remember at the time, and I told him what the first defendant said. Still Tweedledee was unable to solve the case."

"This is most interesting!" said Alice. "So, knowing that Tweedledee couldn't solve the case, knowing what you told him, then I should be able to solve the case?"

"Oh, no," replied the Knight, "there is more to come!

"A week later," continued the Knight, "I met Tweedledum. I didn't tell him about my meeting with Tweedledee, but I told him everything else I've told you so far. Then Tweedledum wanted to know, not what the first defendant said, but he either asked me what the second defendant had said, or else he asked me what the

third defendant had said, but today I unfortunately cannot remember which question he asked me. Anyhow, whichever question he asked me, I knew the answer at the time and told him. Still, Tweedledum was unable to solve the case."

"This gets more intriguing by the minute," replied Alice. "So now I have enough information to solve the case?"

"Oh, no," replied the Knight, "I must yet tell you more.

"Well," he continued, "only last week I met Humpty Dumpty and told him everything I've told you so far. I told him all about the Jabberwocky solving the case and all about the fact that neither Tweedledee nor Tweedledum could solve it, even with the added information they had. Humpty Dumpty immediately took out his pencil and notebook and worked on it quite a while. Finally, he shook his head and said, 'I don't have enough data! If only you could remember whether it was the second defendant or the third defendant whom Tweedledum inquired about, then I *might* be able to solve it—but even then, I'm not sure that I could.' Well, fortunately, I *did* remember at the time, and I told Humpty Dumpty which of the two defendants Tweedledum inquired about. I didn't tell Humpty Dumpty what that defendant said, because I didn't remember at the time, but I did tell him which defendant it was. From this, Humpty Dumpty was able to solve the case.

"And now," concluded the White Knight, "I have given you enough information for *you* to solve the case."

"Alice could *really* solve this case?" asked Alice in astonishment.

"Yes, she could," I replied, "and so can you. Only it involves a good deal of concentration!"

Who was guilty?

## CHAPTER 10

# *Looking-Glass Logic*

Lewis Carroll has told us very little about the other White Knight; all he told us was that he once tried to put on the first White Knight's helmet, which was very careless, considering that the first White Knight was in it at the time.

Well, when Alice met him, she was totally baffled! So many statements he made seemed to be wrong! Could he be one of those people who always lie? thought Alice. No, she rejected this outright, since her intuition told her that he was a completely sincere person. But the things he said! First of all he told Alice that she was a unicorn. When Alice asked him, "Do you really believe I am a unicorn?" he answered, "No." Next he claimed that the White King was asleep and dreaming of Alice, but then he said the White King was not dreaming of anything. Then two contradictory statements came up (I forget just what they were) and he first claimed that one of them was true, then he claimed the other was false, and then he claimed that they were both true.

At first, Alice thought that he was simply being inconsistent, but she could never catch him in a direct inconsistency—that is, she could find no statement which he claimed to be true and also claimed to be false, though he would claim that the statement was both true and false! Still, she could not get him to make separate claims—one that the statement was true, and the other that the statement was false.

After several hours of questioning, Alice gatered an enormous amount of data, which she recorded in her memorandum book. She took it all to Humpty Dumpty to see if he could explain it.

"It figures," said Humpty Dumpty, looking through Alice's notes, "it figures!"

"What do you mean by that?" asked Alice. "Is this White Knight untruthful?"

"The White Knights never lie," replied Humpty Dumpty.

"Then I don't understand," replied Alice, "I really don't understand!"

"Of course not," responded Humpty Dumpty contemptuously, "you don't understand Looking-Glass logic!"

"And what is Looking-Glass logic?"

"The kind of logic used by Looking-Glass logicians," he replied.

"And what is a Looking-Glass logician?" asked Alice.

"Why, one who uses Looking-Glass logic," he replied. "Surely, you could have guessed *that!*"

Alice thought this over. Somehow, she didn't find this explanation very helpful.

"You see," he continued, "there are certain people here called Looking-Glass logicians. Their statements seem a bit bizarre until you understand the key—which is really quite simple. Once the key is understood, the whole business makes perfect sense."

"And what is the key?" asked Alice, more curious than ever.

"Oh, it would never do to *tell* you the key! However, I will give you some clues. In fact, I will give you the five basic conditions about Looking-Glass logicians from which you can *deduce* the key. Here are the conditions:

*"Condition One*—A Looking-Glass logician is completely honest. He will claim those and only those statements which he actually believes.

*"Condition Two*—Whenever a Looking-Glass logician claims a statement to be true, then he also claims that he doesn't believe the statement."

"Just a minute," interrupted Alice. "Are you not contradicting yourself? According to the first condition, a Looking-Glass logician is always truthful. If, then, he claims a statement to be true, he must really believe that it is true. How then, without lying, can he claim that he doesn't believe the statement?"

"Good question," replied Humpty Dumpty. "However, I never said that a Looking-Glass logician is always *accurate*! Just because he believes something doesn't mean that he necessarily *knows* that he believes it, nor even that he necessarily believes that he believes it. Indeed, it could happen that he erroneously believes that he doesn't believe it."

"You mean," replied Alice, utterly astonished, "that a person can actually believe something, and yet believe that he doesn't believe it?"

"With Looking-Glass logicians, yes," replied Humpty Dumpty, "in fact with Looking-Glass logicians this *always* happens—this is a direct consequence of the first two conditions."

"How is that?" asked Alice.

"Well," replied Humpty Dumpty, "suppose he believes a statement to be true. Then, by Condition One, he claims the statement is

*116*

true. Then, by Condition Two, he claims that he doesn't believe the statement. Hence, again by Condition One, he must believe that he doesn't believe the statement.

"Anyhow," continued Humpty Dumpty, "I'm giving you too many hints! Let me finish my list of conditions, and then you should deduce the key to the entire mystery.

"*Condition Three*—Given any true statement, he (the Looking-Glass logician) always claims that he believes the statement.

"*Condition Four*—If a Looking-Glass logician believes something, then he cannot also believe its opposite.

"*Condition Five*—Given any statement, a Looking-Glass logician either believes the statement or he believes its opposite.

"And that," concluded Humpty Dumpty proudly, "is the entire list of conditions. From these you should be able to infer just which statements a Looking-Glass logician believes to be true and just which ones he believes to be false. I will now ask you some questions to test your understanding.

"*Question One*—Suppose a Looking-Glass logician believes that the Red King is asleep. Does he believe that the Red King is dreaming of you, or doesn't he?"

"Now, how could I possibly know that?" cried Alice.

"You should," replied Humpty Dumpty. "The answer follows directly from the conditions, but I won't tell you how until later. Meanwhile, let me ask you this:

"*Question Two*—Suppose a Looking-Glass logician believes that either the Red King or the Red Queen is asleep. Does it follow that he believes that the Red Queen is asleep?"

"Why should it?" replied Alice.

"It does," said Humpty Dumpty, "but I won't tell you why till later. Meanwhile, try this:

"*Question Three*—Suppose he (the Looking-Glass logician) believes that the Red King is asleep. Does he necessarily believe that the Red Queen is asleep?"

"Now, why in the world should he?" asked Alice, more bewildered than ever.

"Good question," replied Humpty Dumpty, "and we'll discuss it later. Meanwhile, try this:

"*Question Four*—Suppose he believes that the Red King is asleep. Does he necessarily believe that the Red King and the Red Queen are both asleep?"

"Isn't that the same question as the last?" asked Alice. "If he believes the Red King to be asleep, then isn't it the same thing believing the Red Queen is asleep as believing both are asleep?"

"Not at all," replied Humpty Dumpty decidedly.

"Why not?" asked Alice.

"I'll tell you later," replied Humpty Dumpty. "Meanwhile, try this:

"*Question Five*—Suppose he believes the Red King and the Red Queen are both asleep. Does it follow that he believes the Red King is asleep?"

"I imagine it would," replied Alice.

"It doesn't!" said Humpty Dumpty. "Here, try this one:

"*Question Six*—"Suppose he believes that the Red King and the Red Queen are either both asleep or both awake. Does it follow that he believes of one of them that he or she is asleep and of the other that he or she is awake?"

"Of course not!" said Alice.

"It *does* follow!" said Humpty Dumpty, "but I won't tell you why till later. Here, try this one:

"*Question Seven*—Suppose he believes that the Lion is not in the forest unless the Unicorn is with him. Does he believe that the Lion is in the forest or doesn't he?"

"I see no way to tell!" replied Alice.

"Of course not," replied Humpty Dumpty contemptuously, "you don't yet have the key! Well, try this one:

"*Question Eight*—Suppose he believes that the Jabberwocky has made at least one true statement in his life. Does it follow that he believes every statement the Jabberwocky ever made?"

"Now, why should it?" asked Alice. "This sounds plain silly!"

"It *does* follow," said Humpty Dumpty, "but I think I'm giving you too many hints! Well, let's see if you can get this:

"*Question Nine*—Suppose he believes that all gryphons have wings. Does it follow that there are any gryphons?"

"I'm totally confused by all this!" cried Alice. "I have no idea what Looking-Glass logic is all about!"

"Well, try this," said Humpty Dumpty.

"*Question Ten*—Suppose he believes that Alice will not reach the eighth square without becoming a queen. Suppose he also believes that Alice will reach the eighth square. Does he believe that Alice will become a queen, or doesn't he?"

"I guess he does," replied Alice, "doesn't he?"

"Well," said Humpty Dumpty, laughing, "the last question was really kind of unfair, so I don't expect you to get it."

"More unfair than the other questions?" asked Alice.

"Decidedly," he replied, "the other questions were all perfectly fair."

"I find them *all* equally confusing!" replied Alice, "I still don't understand this Looking-Glass logic!"

Now, if *you*, like Alice, are confused at this point, I can hardly blame you! Yet the key to the whole mystery is almost laughably simple. Rather than give a solution section to this chapter, I will incorporate the solutions in the dialogue which now follows.

### Humpty Dumpty Explains It

"Well," said Humpty, "it's high time you tried to figure out the key!"

"I have no idea where even to begin!"

"Consider this," said Humpty Dumpty. "Is it possible for a Looking-Glass logician to believe a true statement?"

"Why not?" asked Alice.

"Well, do you recall what I proved to you before—that whenever a Looking-Glass logician believes something, then he also believes that he doesn't believe it?"

"Ye-es," said Alice, "but I've forgotten the proof; could you please go over it again?"

"Surely," he replied. "Take any statement that a Looking-Glass logician believes. Since he believes the statement, then he claims the statement (by Condition One), hence he claims that he doesn't believe it (by Condition Two), hence he believes he doesn't believe it (by Condition One)."

"Oh, yes," said Alice, "now I remember!"

"Well, to be sure you will continue to remember, I want you to write it down in your memorandum book and label it as Proposition One."

So Alice wrote the following:

> *Proposition 1*—Whenever a Looking-Glass logician believes something, then he believes that he doesn't believe it.

"The next thing to realize," said Humpty Dumpty, "is that given any true statement, a Looking-Glass logician believes that he *does* believe the statement."

"Why is that?" asked Alice.

"Oh, that is easy to prove!" replied Humpty Dumpty: "Take any true statement. By Condition Three, he claims to believe the statement. Since he claims to believe it, and he is honest (Conditon One), then he believes that he believes it."

"I see," said Alice.

"Better write that down, and label it as Proposition Two," suggested Humty Dumpty.

So Alice wrote the following:

> *Proposition 2*—Given any true statement, a Looking-Glass logician believes that he believes the statement.

"Now," said Humpty Dumpty, "do you see why it is impossible for a Looking-Glass logician ever to believe a true statement?"

"Not quite," admitted Alice.

"This follows easily from Proposition One, Proposition Two, and Condition Four," he replied. "Take any statement that a Looking-Glass logician believes. By Proposition One, he believes that he doesn't believe the statement. Then he can't also believe that he *does* believe the statement (because by Condition Four he can never believe anything and also believe its opposite). Since he doesn't believe that he believes it, then the statement cannot be true, for if it *were* true, then by Proposition Two he *would* believe that he believes it. But he *doesn't* believe that he believes it—therefore it can't be true. So, you see, a Looking-Glass logician never believes any true statement; all things believed by a Looking-Glass logician are false."

Alice pondered over this for some time. "That's a rather difficult proof!" she said.

"Oh, you'll get used to it in time!"

Alice thought some more about this. "Tell me something else," said Alice. "Does a Looking-Glass logician necessarily believe all false statements, or is it just that he believes only false statements?"

"That's a good question, child," replied Humpty Dumpty, "and the answer is yes. Take any false statement. By Condition Five, he either believes the statement or he believes its opposite. He can't believe its opposite, because its opposite is true! Therefore he believes the false statement."

"How extraordinary!" exclaimed Alice. "So a Looking-Glass logician believes *all* false statements and no true ones!"

"Exactly," said Humpty Dumpty, "and that's the beautiful part of it!"

"Another interesting thing," added Humpty Dumpty, "is that anyone who believes all false statements and no true ones, and who is also honest in expressing his beliefs—any such person must satisfy the five basic conditions which characterize Looking-Glass logicians."

"Why is that?" asked Alice.

"Oh, that's very easy to prove!" replied Humpty Dumpty. "Suppose a person is completely honest and also believes all and only those statements which are false. Since he is honest, then of course he satisfies Condition One. As for Condition Two, suppose he claims a statement to be true. Then he really believes the statement (because he is honest). Therefore it is false that he doesn't believe the statement. But he believes *everything* that is false—even false things about his own beliefs! So, since it is false that he doesn't believe the statement, and since he believes everything which is false, then he must believe the false fact that he doesn't believe the statement—in other words, he believes that he doesn't believe the statement. And since he *believes* that he doesn't believe the statement, then he *claims* he doesn't believe it (because, we recall, he is honest). Therefore he satisfies Condition Two.

"As for Condition Three, take any true statement. Since it is true, he cannot believe it. Since he *doesn't* believe it, then he must believe that he *does* believe it (because all his beliefs are wrong!). Then, since he believes that he believes it, then he must claim that he believes it (again, since he is honest). This proves that he satisfies Condition Three.

"Conditions Four and Five are obvious," continued Humpty Dumpty. "Take any statement and its opposite. One of them must be true and the other must be false. Therefore he believes the false one and doesn't believe the true one. So he doesn't believe both of them, hence he satisfies Condition Four, but he believes at least one of them, so he satisfies Condition Five.

"And that," concluded Humpty Dumpty, "is the entire story: A Looking-Glass logician is honest but totally deluded. Conversely, anyone who is both honest and totally deluded satisfies the five conditions of being a Looking-Glass logician. Now you have the key."

"One thing still puzzles me," said Alice. "Why is it that a Looking-Glass logician never claims any statement and also claims its opposite, and yet he will claim that the statement and its opposite are both true?"

"That's easy," replied Humpty Dumpty. "Take, for example, the statement that the Red King is asleep. Its opposite is that the Red King is awake. Clearly one of them is true and the other false. The Looking-Glass logician believes only the one which is false, hence he can't believe each of them separately. Yet the *single* statement that the Red King is both asleep and awake is a false statement, hence the Looking-Glass logician must believe this false statement.

"And now that you have the key, the answers to my ten questions should all be obvious."

Here are the answers that Humpty Dumpty gave to his ten questions:

*1*—Since the Looking-Glass logician believes the Red King is asleep, then the Red King must actually be awake. Therefore the Red King is not dreaming of Alice. (By dreaming, I don't mean daydreaming!) Since the King is not dreaming of Alice, then the Looking-Glass logician must believe that he *is* dreaming of Alice.

*2*—Since he (the Looking-Glass logician) believes that either the Red King or the Red Queen is asleep, then it is false that either the Red King or the Red Queen is asleep. This means that both of them are actually awake. Since the Red Queen is awake, then he must believe that she is asleep. (By the same token he must also believe that the Red King is asleep.)

*3*—He believes the Red King is asleep, which merely means that the Red King is awake. This tells us nothing about whether the Red Queen is asleep or not, so we have no way of knowing whether he believes she is asleep.

*4*—This is a different story! Since he believes that the Red King is asleep, then it is false that the Red King is asleep. Hence it is certainly false that the Red King and Queen are both asleep! Therefore he must believe that they are both asleep.

So the curious thing is that he doesn't necessarily believe that the Red Queen is asleep, yet he does believe that the Red King and the Red Queen are both asleep!

*5*—He believes they are both asleep, from which only follows that at least one is awake. We don't know which one, hence we cannot determine whether or not the Looking-Glass logician believes the King is asleep.

*6*—Since he believes that they are either both asleep or both

125

awake, then it is not true that they are either both asleep or both awake. This means that one of them is asleep and the other is awake. The one who's sleeping he believes is awake, and the one who's awake he believes is asleep.

7—Since his belief is wrong, then in fact the Lion must be in the forest without the Unicorn. Therefore the Lion is in the forest. So he must believe that the Lion is not in the forest.

8—Since his belief is false, then the Jabberwocky has never made any true statements in his life; all statements ever made by the Jabberwocky have been false. Therefore the Looking-Glass logician must believe every one of them!

9—Since he believes that all gryphons have wings, then it is false that all gryphons have wings, which means there must be at least one gryphon without wings. Therefore there must be at least one gryphon.

10—This is a trick question, because it is not possible that a Looking-Glass logician can believe both these facts!

Suppose he believes that Alice won't reach the eighth square without becoming a queen. Then it is false that Alice won't reach the eighth square without becoming a queen, which means that Alice will reach the eighth square without becoming a queen. Hence it is true that Alice will reach the eighth square, so it is impossible that the Looking-Glass logician can believe that she will.

## CHAPTER 11

# The Red King's Theory

At this point Alice's conversation with Humpty Dumpty was interrupted by a strange rumbling sound in the distance—something like the puffing of a steam engine.

"What is that?" asked Alice, in some alarm.

"Oh, that's only the Red King snoring," replied Humpty Dumpty. "You should go have a look at him—he's quite a sight!"

"Oh, yes," said Alice, remembering her very first journey into the Looking-Glass, "I've seen him asleep once before; I was with Tweedledum and Tweedledee at the time, and they told me that the Red King was dreaming of *me* and that I was nothing more than a thing in his dream, and if he were to awaken, I wouldn't exist anymore. Now, wasn't that a foolish thing to have said?"

"Why don't you try waking him and find out?" replied Humpty Dumpty.

"I've half a mind to!" replied Alice defiantly. "Only it would be rather inconsiderate, you know!"

"I *don't* know," replied Humpty Dumpty. "Anyway, you can go have a look at him if you like; I wish to remain here and work on some more logic puzzles."

At this hint Alice thought she should depart. After thanking Humpty Dumpty for his instructive logic lesson, she made her way into the wood in the direction of the snoring.

When she came upon the Red King, he was just waking up, and Tweedledum and Tweedledee were standing close by, watching him.

"So the King is awake!" cried Alice to the Tweedle brothers. "And I still exist as much as I did before. What do you have to say to that!" she added triumphantly.

"I think we better get back to the house," said Tweedledee to his brother. "It might rain any minute. *You* can stay here if you like," he said to Alice, "but my brother and I must be getting back, you know."

Alice looked up, but there was not a cloud in the sky.

"I think I will stay," said Alice. "I would like to have a talk with the Red King. But I do wish to thank you again for those delightful logic games. I enjoyed them thoroughly!"

Arm in arm, the two brothers slowly sauntered out of the wood.

After watching them for a while, Alice turned to the Red King, who was by now thoroughly awake.

"You must be *Alice*!" said the King.

"Why, yes," Alice replied, "only how did you know?"

"Oh," replied the King, "I just had the strangest dream! I dreamed that I was walking through the woods with Tweedledee and Tweedledum, and we came across a girl who looked *exactly* like you, curled up fast asleep against a tree. 'Who is that?' I asked. 'Why, that is *Alice*,' said Tweedledee, 'and do you know what she is dreaming about?' I replied, 'How could anyone know what she is dreaming about?' 'Why, she is dreaming about *you*!' he replied. Then both brothers tried to convince me that I had no independent existence of my own but that I was only an idea in your mind and that if you were to wake up, I'd go out—bang!—just like a candle!

"So now," continued the King, "I'm certainly glad to see you awake and to see that I have *not* gone out—bang!—just like a candle!"

"How utterly extraordinary!" cried Alice. "Why, the very same thing happened in reverse the first time I ever saw you: You were asleep, I was with Tweedledee and Tweedledum, and they told me that you were dreaming about me and that if you were to awaken, *I* would no longer exist but go out—bang!—like a candle!"

"Well, we're both awake and neither of us has gone out—bang!—like a candle," replied the King with a smile. "So it seems that the Tweedle brothers were either mistaken or just trying to tease us!"

"How do I know for sure that I'm awake?" asked Alice. "Why can't it be that I'm now asleep and dreaming all this?"

"Ah, that's an interesting question and one quite difficult to answer!" replied the King. "I once had a long philosophical discussion with Humpty Dumpty about this. Do you know him?"

"Oh, yes!" replied Alice.

"Well, Humpty Dumpty is one of the keenest arguers I know—he can convince just about anyone of just about anything when he puts his mind to it! Anyway, he *almost* had me convinced that I had no valid reason to be sure that I was awake, but I outsmarted him! It took me about three hours, but I finally convinced him that I *must* be awake, and so he conceded that I had won the argument. And then—"

The King did not finish his sentence but stood lost in thought.

"And then *what*?" asked Alice.

"And then I woke up!" said the King, a bit sheepishly.

"Oh, then Humpty Dumpty was right after all!" cried Alice.

"Right about *what*?" asked the King. "I never really had this conversation with Humpty Dumpty; I only *dreamed* that I did!"

"I didn't mean the *real* Humpty Dumpty," replied Alice. "I meant the Humpty Dumpty you dreamed about. It was *he* who was right!"

"Now, just a minute!" said the King, "what are you trying to tell me—that there are *two* Humpty Dumptys, one the real one and the other the one I dreamed about?"

Alice did not quite know what to say to this.

"Anyway," said the King, "in the meantime, I have thought of a much better argument proving that I am awake—this argument couldn't *possibly* be wrong; it *must* be right!"

"Now, *that* I should like to hear!" said Alice.

"Well," said the King, "to begin with, I hold the theory that everyone in the world is of one of two types: Type A or Type B. Those of Type A are totally accurate in their beliefs while they are awake, but totally inaccurate while they are asleep. Everything they believe while they are awake is true, but everything they believe while they are asleep is false. People of Type B are the reverse: Everything they believe while they are asleep is true, and everything they believe while awake is false."

"What an extraordinary theory!" said Alice. "But what proof do you have that it is correct?"

"Oh, I will later prove to you beyond any reasonable doubt that it *is* correct, but for the time being, I want you to realize some of the consequences of the theory. To begin with, the following two propositions follow immediately:

"*Proposition One*—If, at a given time, a person believes he is awake, then he must be of Type A.

"*Proposition Two*—If, at a given time, a person believes he is of Type A, then he must be awake at that time."

The King then proved these two propositions to Alice's satisfaction; at least Alice could find no flaw in the arguments.

♛88

A QUESTION Do Propositions 1 and 2 really follow from the Red King's theory?

\*    \*    \*

"Now that you understand the proofs of Propositions One and Two," continued the King, "you are ready for the proof that I am now awake."

## The Red King's Proof

"I shall prove three things," said the King. "I shall prove: (one) I am of Type A; (two) I am awake; (three) my theory is correct.

"To begin with, you must accept as premiss that I *believe* these three things. Do you grant me that?"

"Oh, certainly," replied Alice, "I don't for a moment doubt that you *believe* these things; the only question in my mind is whether they are really true!"

"From the fact that I believe them," said the King, "it follows that they *must* be true!"

"What!" said Alice in astonishment. "Are you saying that because someone *believes* something, it follows that it must be true?"

"Of course not!" cried the King. "I know as well as you do that just because someone believes something, it does not necessarily mean that it is true. However, these three particular things have the remarkable property that believing all three of them *makes* them true!"

"How can that be?" asked Alice.

"That's what I am about to prove to you!" said the King. "Now, child, attend carefully: Since I believe I am awake, then I must be of Type A."

"That follows from Proposition One," said Alice.

"Exactly!" replied the King. "And by Proposition Two, since I believe I am of Type A, then I must now be awake."

"Yes," said Alice.

"Very well then," concluded the King triumphantly, "since I am both awake and of Type A, then my present beliefs must all be correct. Since my present beliefs are correct and I believe the theory I have propounded, then the theory *is* true! What better proof could you have than that?"

CHAPTER ♛ 12

# *Which Alice?*

"Now, just a minute," said Michael, "you don't expect me to believe the Red King's theory, do you?"

"Why not?" I replied, scarcely able to restrain a smile.

"It's the most ridiculous theory I ever heard in my life!"

"Why?" I asked. "Isn't the theory logically possible?"

"Of course not!" cried Michael. "The whole theory is crazy from beginning to end!"

"But the King *proved* that his theory was correct, didn't he?" I asked.

There was a long, thoughtful pause. Alice was the first to break the silence.

"Not really," she said, "the Red King's proof was fallacious."

"Just where was the fallacy?" I innocently inquired.

"The entire argument was circular," replied Alice. "The proofs that a person who believes he is of Type A must be awake, and that a person who believes he is awake must be of Type A—these proofs depend on the theory being correct in the first place!"

"Very good!" I replied. "That's exactly the fallacy!"

"So I was right!" exclaimed Michael. "The theory *is* false!"

"No, no!" I sharply corrected. "Alice didn't prove that the theory is false; she merely proved that the Red King failed to prove that the theory is true. But just because the King's proof was wrong doesn't mean that the theory itself is wrong."

"It's the silliest theory I ever heard!" said Michael quite emphatically.

"Silly is one thing; logically impossible is another," I answered. "I grant that the theory is highly improbable, but that does not mean that the theory is logically impossible.

"And there is something about the King's argument worth observing," I added, "namely that if the King himself were of either Type A or Type B, then his believing those three things *would* make them true! The King's argument would be valid if we added the premiss that the King is of Type A or Type B; if the King is of one of those two types, it really follows that everyone else is—in other words that the theory must be correct."

"I still think it's the stupidest theory I ever heard," said Michael, and that appeared to be the end of the matter.

But it was not quite the end of the matter! That night Alice had a remarkable dream. When she went to bed, her mind was filled with all the strange puzzles she had heard that day—particularly the inversion of truth and falsity of the Looking-Glass logicians, and the Red King's theory.

Is it really possible that the Red King's theory could be correct? thought Alice. And if so, I wonder which type I would be, Type A or Type B?

Then Alice had the dream. She dreamed that she was the other Alice—the Alice in the Looking-Glass. She dreamed that she met the Red King and explained to him the gap in his proof. He then filled in the gap by giving her another proof that he really was either of Type A or Type B. (Unfortunately, Alice couldn't remember the proof the next morning, so I can't tell *you* what it was!) Anyway, Alice was thoroughly convinced in her sleep that the King really was of Type A or Type B, and hence (by the King's first argument) that everybody was of Type A or Type B. Then they had the following conversation:

"There is another Alice," said the King, "who right now is asleep and who is dreaming she is you."

"How extraordinary!" exclaimed Alice. "Isn't it possible that it is *I* who am now asleep and dreaming I am she?"

"It comes to the same thing," replied the King.

This remark puzzled Alice dreadfully! She could not see at all *why* it was the same thing.

"Which Alice do you think you are?" asked the King.

"At this point, I hardly know!" she replied.

"Are you of Type A or Type B?" asked the King.

"I'm afraid I don't know that either," replied Alice. "In fact, right now I am not sure whether I am asleep or awake."

"Well, let me test you," said the King. "What color are your eyes?"

"Why, they're brown, of course— Oh, no, I think they're blue! Now wait, it depends on which Alice I really am. Which Alice am I, and what color are my eyes?"

"Well, let me put it this way," replied the King. "The Jabberwocky happens to know about you and the other Alice. When he's asleep he believes that one of you has brown eyes and that the other one has blue eyes. When he's awake, he believes that you have brown eyes and that the other Alice has blue eyes. Now can you tell me the color of your eyes?"

Well, dear readers, I shall leave this little puzzle with you to solve all on your own. What color eyes does my friend Alice have, and what about the other Alice? A second problem: What type is the Jabberwocky?

# SOLUTIONS
# TO THE PUZZLES

## Chapter 1

WHICH ONE IS JOHN? To find out which brother is John, ask one of them, "Is John truthful?" If he answers yes, then he must be John, regardless of whether he is lying or telling the truth. If he answers no, then the other one is John. This can be proven in the following manner.

If he answers yes, he is asserting that John is truthful. If his assertion is true, then John really is truthful, and since the speaker is being truthful, he must be John. If his assertion is a lie, then John is not really truthful; John then lies just like the speaker, hence again the speaker must be John. This proves that regardless of whether the speaker is telling the truth or lying, he must be John (assuming he answers yes).

If he answers no, he is asserting that John is not truthful. If his assertion is true, then John is not truthful; if his assertion is a lie, then John *is* truthful. In either case the speaker is unlike John, hence must be John's brother. Thus a No answer indicates that the speaker is not John.

Of course, the question "Does John lie?" serves equally well: A Yes answer then indicates that the speaker is *not* John, and a No answer indicates that he is John.

These are the only three-word questions I can think of that must work. I wonder if there are any others?

* * *

For the second puzzle—to find a question that will determine whether John lies—you have merely to ask, "Are you John?"

Suppose he answers yes. Either he is telling the truth or he isn't. Suppose he is. Then he really is John, and since he is telling the truth, John is truthful. On the other hand, suppose he is lying. Then he is not really John (since he is claiming he is). Then he is lying and is not John, so John must be the truthful brother. This proves that if he answers yes, then, regardless of whether he is lying or telling the truth, John must be truthful.

Suppose he answers no. Either he is lying or telling the truth. Suppose he is telling the truth. Then he really isn't John; John must be the other brother, and (since he is telling the truth), John must be the one who lies. On the other hand, suppose he is lying. Then (since he is claiming not to be John), he must be John, and so in this case John lies. This proves that if he answers no, then, regardless of whether he is telling the truth or lying, John must be the one who lies.

There is a pretty symmetry between the solutions to these two puzzles: To find out whether he (the one addressed) is John, you ask, "Does John lie?" To find out whether John lies, you ask, "Are you John?"

## Chapter 2

✦1

THE FIRST TALE  The Hatter said, in effect, that either the March Hare or the Dormouse stole it. If the Hatter lied, then neither the March Hare nor the Dormouse stole it, which means that the March Hare didn't steal it, hence was speaking the truth. Therefore, if the Hatter lied, then the March Hare didn't lie, so it is impossible that the Hatter and the March Hare both lied. Therefore the Dormouse spoke the truth when he said that the Hatter and March Hare didn't both lie. So we know that the Dormouse spoke the truth. But we are given that the Dormouse and the March Hare didn't both speak the truth. Then, since the Dormouse did, the March Hare didn't. This means that the March Hare lied, so his statement was false, which means that the March Hare stole the jam.

### ♛2

THE SECOND TALE   Suppose the March Hare stole it. Since the thief told the truth, this would mean that the March Hare's claim was true—in other words that the Hatter stole it. But we are given that only one creature stole it, so it is not possible that the March Hare stole it. Therefore the March Hare is innocent, but we are given that both innocent ones lied, therefore the March Hare lied. So it is not true that the Hatter stole it (as the March Hare claimed). So neither the March Hare nor the Hatter stole it, so it must be the Dormouse who stole it.

### ♛3

THE THIRD TALE   If the Duchess had stolen the pepper, she would certainly have known it, hence she would have told the truth when she said that she knew who stole the pepper. But we are given that people who steal pepper never tell the truth. Therefore the Duchess must be innocent.

### ♛4

SO, WHO STOLE THE PEPPER?   If the March Hare stole the pepper, then he lied (because people who steal pepper always lie), hence his statement about the Hatter would be false, which would mean that the Hatter also stole the pepper. But we are given that no more than one creature stole the pepper. Therefore the March Hare couldn't have stolen the pepper. Since the March Hare is innocent, then he told the truth—therefore what he said about the Hatter was true, so the Hatter is also innocent. Therefore the Hatter also told the truth, which means that the Dormouse is also innocent. So none of the three suspects stole the pepper.

♛5

THEN WHO *DID* STEAL THE PEPPER? Suppose the Gryphon were guilty. Then he lied, which means the Mock Turtle is not innocent (like the Gryphon said) but is guilty, so we would have two guilty ones, which we don't have (as mentioned in the last problem). Therefore the Gryphon is innocent. So his statement is true, hence the Mock Turtle is innocent. Therefore the Mock Turtle's statement is true, so the Lobster is guilty.

♛6

A METAPUZZLE For those who know the book, the Lobster (unlike the Gryphon and the Mock Turtle) never really appeared in *Alice in Wonderland*—rather he was a character in one of the *poems* recited by Alice.

♛7

THE FOURTH TALE Suppose the Duchess stole the sugar. Then she lied, which means that what she said about the Cook not stealing the sugar was false—in other words the Cook must have also stolen the sugar. But we are given that only one person stole the sugar. So it is impossible that the Duchess stole it. Therefore the Cook stole the sugar. (Incidentally, both must have been lying.)

♛8

THE FIFTH TALE If the Cheshire Cat ate the salt, then all three are lying, so this possibility is out. If Bill ate the salt, then all three are telling the truth, so this possibility is out. Therefore the Caterpillar must have eaten the salt (hence also the first two statements are lies and the third is the truth).

♛9

THE SIXTH TALE If the Frog-Footman stole it, then he and the Knave both lied, so this is out. If the Fish-Footman stole it, then he and the Knave both lied, so this is out. Therefore the Knave of Hearts stole it (and, humorously enough, he told the truth—and so did the Fish-Footman).

### ♛ 10

THE SEVENTH TALE   It is impossible that the Cheshire Cat stole it, because the thief would then be telling the truth. Therefore the Cheshire Cat didn't steal it (and the Cat and the Duchess were both lying). If the Cook stole it, then all three would be lying, which is contrary to what was given. Therefore the Duchess stole it (and hence the Duchess is lying, the Cheshire Cat is lying, and the Cook is telling the truth).

### ♛ 11

THE SEVENTH TALE (CONTINUED)   Again, the Cheshire Cat couldn't have stolen it for the same reason as the last problem. Suppose the Duchess stole it. Then the Cat is lying and the Cook is telling the truth—which contradicts the given fact that if the Duchess stole it, the other two are either both lying or both telling the truth. Therefore the Duchess didn't steal it, so the Cook did. (And the other two are both lying or both telling the truth—in fact they are both lying. In fact all three are lying.)

### ♛ 12

THE EIGHTH TALE   To begin with, the Dormouse couldn't have stolen the butter, becasue if he had, he would be telling the truth—which would mean he stole the milk. So the Dormouse didn't steal the butter. Therefore the March Hare or the Hatter stole the butter. If the March Hare stole the butter, then his statement about the Hatter would be true (remember, the one who stole the butter told the truth), which would mean that the Hatter stole the butter, but it is not possible that both stole the butter. Therefore the March Hare didn't steal the butter. This means that the Hatter stole the butter. Therefore his statement was true, which means that the Dormouse stole the eggs. This means also that the March Hare stole the milk.

So the March Hare stole the milk; the Hatter stole the butter (and told the truth); and the Dormouse stole the eggs (and lied).

♛13

THE FINAL TALE If the White Rabbit had known a little more logic, he could never have said that Bill was right and the Knave was wrong, because it is logically impossible that Bill could be right and the Knave could be wrong! In other words, I am saying that if Bill is right, then the Knave *has* to be right. Let me prove this.

Suppose Bill the Lizard is right. Then what he said is true, which means that either the March Hare or the Dormouse is right (or possibly both). Suppose the March Hare is right. Then the Cook must be right (because the March Hare said that the Cook and the Cheshire Cat are both right). On the other hand, if the Dormouse is right, then again the Cook is right (because the Dormouse said so). So in either case (whether the March Hare or the Dormouse is right) the Cook must be right. But either the March Hare or the Dormouse is right. Therefore the Cook must be right in either case. This proves that the Cook is right (assuming, of course, that the Lizard was right, which we are doing). Also, the March Hare said that the Cheshire Cat (as well as the Cook) is right, and the Dormouse said that the Caterpillar (as well as the Cook) is right. Therefore either the Cheshire Cat or the Caterpillar is right (because either the March Hare or the Dormouse is right: if the former, the Cheshire Cat is right; if the latter, the Caterpillar is right). Well, the Hatter said that either the Cheshire Cat or the Caterpillar is right, so the Hatter is right. This means that the Cook and Hatter are both right—which is exactly what the Knave of Hearts said! So the Knave of Hearts is right (all providing, of course, that Bill is right).

So we have proved that if Bill the Lizard is right, then the Knave of Hearts must be right. Therefore the White Rabbit was quite wrong when he said that Bill was right and the Knave was wrong. So the Rabbit was wrong.

Now we use Alice's statement (which is given to be true) which is that the White Rabbit and the Duchess are either both right or both wrong. They can't be both right (since the Rabbit was not right), hence they must be both wrong. Since the Duchess was wrong, then the Gryphon must have stolen the tarts.

## Chapter 3

### ⚜14

THE CATERPILLAR AND THE LIZARD  The Caterpillar believes that he and the Lizard are both mad. If the Caterpillar were sane, it would be false that he and the Lizard were both mad, hence the Caterpillar (being sane) couldn't possibly believe this false fact. Therefore the Caterpillar must be mad. Since he is mad, his belief is wrong, so it is not true that *both* are mad. So the other one (the Lizard) must be sane. Therefore the Caterpillar is mad and the Lizard is sane.

### ⚜15

THE COOK AND THE CAT  If the Cook were mad, then it would be true that at least one of the two is mad, and we would have a mad person holding a true belief, which is not possible. Therefore the Cook must be sane. Since she is sane, her belief is correct, hence one of the two really is mad. Since it is not the Cook, it must be the Cheshire Cat. Therefore the Cook is sane and the Cheshire Cat is mad.

### ⚜16

THE FISH-FOOTMAN AND THE FROG-FOOTMAN  It is impossible to determine from the given facts whether the Fish-Footman is sane or mad, but we will prove that the Frog-Footman must be sane. We prove this as follows:

There are two possibilities: Either the Fish-Footman is sane or he is mad. We will show that in either case the Frog-Footman must be sane.

Suppose the Fish-Footman is sane. Then his belief is correct, which means that the Frog-Footman really is like the Fish-Footman, which means the Frog-Footman is sane.

On the other hand, suppose the Fish-Footman is mad. Then his belief is wrong, so the Frog-Footman is the opposite of the Fish-Footman. Since the Fish-Footman is mad and the Frog-Footman is the opposite, the Frog-Footman must be sane.

We therefore see that in either case (whether the Fish-Footman is sane or whether he is mad) the Frog-Footman must be sane.

Incidentally, if the Fish-Footman had believed that the Frog-Footman was opposite to him, rather than like him, what would this have made the Frog-Footman?

*Answer:* The Frog-Footman would have had to be mad. I'll leave this as an exercise for you to prove.


### 17

THE KING AND THE QUEEN OF DIAMONDS    It is impossible that anyone in this setup could believe he or she is mad, because a sane person would know the truth that he is sane, and a mad person would mistakenly believe that he is sane. Therefore the Queen did not really believe she was mad, so the King was mad to believe she did.

Nothing can be deduced about the sanity of the Queen.


### 18

WHAT ABOUT THESE THREE? Suppose the Hatter is sane. Then his belief is correct, which means that the March Hare does not believe that all three are sane. Then the March Hare must be sane, because if he were mad, he would believe the false proposition that all three are sane. Then the Dormouse, believing that the March Hare is sane, must be sane, which makes all three sane. But then how could the sane March Hare fail to believe the true proposition that all three are sane? Therefore it is contradictory to assume the Hatter sane; the Hatter must really be mad.

Since the Hatter is mad, his belief is wrong, and therefore the March Hare does believe that all three are sane. Of course the March Hare is wrong (since the Hatter is not sane), and so the March Hare is also mad. Then the Dormouse, believing the March Hare is sane, is also mad, and so all three are mad (which is not too surprising!).


19


AND THESE THREE? To begin with, the Gryphon and the Mock Turtle must be alike, because the Mock Turtle believes the Gryphon is sane. If the Mock Turtle is sane, his belief is correct, which means that the Gryphon is also sane. If the Mock Turtle is mad, his belief is wrong, which means that the Gryphon is not really sane, but also mad. Therefore the two are alike.

Now I shall prove that the Lobster is mad. Well, suppose he were sane. Then his belief is correct, hence the Gryphon does believe that exactly one of the three is sane. But this is impossible, because if the Gryphon is sane, so is the Mock Turtle (and also the Lobster), so it is false that *exactly* one is sane (all three are), so the sane Gryphon couldn't believe it. On the other hand, if the Gryphon is mad, then it *is* true that exactly one is sane (namely the Lobster, since the Mock Turtle is also mad), but a mad creature can't believe a true statement! Therefore the assumption that the Lobster is sane leads to a contradiction, so the Lobster can't be sane; he must be mad.

Now we know the Lobster is mad. Therefore it is not really true that the Grypon believes that exactly one of the three is sane. If the Gryphon is mad, then the Mock Turtle is also mad, which means that all three are mad, and hence it is false that exactly one of them is sane. This means that the Gryphon, being mad, must believe all false propositions—in particular that exactly one of the three is sane, but we have already proven that he doesn't. This is a contradiction, hence the Gryphon can't be mad. Therefore the Gryphon is sane, and the Mock Turtle (being of the same type as the Gryphon) must also be sane. So the solution is that the Lobster is mad, and the Gryphon and Mock Turtle are both sane.

♛ 20

AND NOW, WHAT ABOUT THESE TWO? The Queen (of Spades) believes that the King believes that she is mad. If she is sane, then the King really does believe she is mad, which means the King must be mad. If she is mad, the King doesn't really believe she is mad, but if he were sane, he would. So in this case, again the King is mad. Therefore in either case, the King must be mad. As for the Queen, she could be either.

*Queen isn't mad. if one deduces from king's statent.*

♛ 21

THE KING AND QUEEN OF CLUBS It is impossible that the King believes the Queen believes the King believes the Queen is mad, for suppose the King did believe this. Suppose the King is sane. Then the Queen really does believe that the King believes she is mad, but as we saw in the last puzzle, this means the King is mad. So if the King is sane, he is mad—therefore the King can't be sane, he is mad. Therefore his belief is false, hence the Queen doesn't really believe that the King believes she is mad. Now, the Queen is either sane or mad. If she is sane, her belief is correct, hence it is true that the King doesn't believe she is mad, so he believes she is sane. Then the King is right, and we have the impossibility of the mad King believing something true. On the other hand, if the Queen is mad, then her belief is wrong, so the King does believe she is mad, which again makes the King sane, which he isn't. So we get a contradiction in either case.

This proves that it simply is not possible that the King believes the Queen believes the King believes she is mad. So, had the Duchess told this to Alice, then *she* would have had to be mad! But, of course, she *didn't* tell this to Alice; all she said was "What would you say *if* I told you—"

♛ 22

AND NOW, WHAT ABOUT THE QUEEN OF HEARTS? What we proved in the last puzzle would apply to the King and Queen of Hearts just as well as the King and Queen of Clubs: It is not possible that the King of Hearts believes that the Queen of Hearts believes that the King of Hearts believes she is mad. Since the Queen of Hearts *does* believe that the King believes this, then she is mad. As for the King, it is not possible from these data to determine what he is.

♛ 23

THE DODO, THE LORY, AND THE EAGLET Since the Lory believes that the Dodo is mad, then the Lory and the Dodo are of opposite types (if the Lory is sane, then the Dodo really is mad; if the Lory is mad, then the Dodo isn't really mad but sane). Since the Eaglet believes that the Dodo is sane, he is opposite to the Lory (who believes the Dodo is mad), hence he is like the Dodo. (Alternatively, one could prove this by reasoning that if the Eaglet is sane, then the Dodo really is sane, and if the Eaglet is mad, then the Dodo is not really sane but mad.) Therefore the Eaglet and the Dodo are alike, and the Lory is opposite to them both. Since the Lory is opposite to the Eaglet, then the Lory must believe that the Eaglet is mad. Therefore the Dodo's belief is correct, so the Dodo is sane. So, the Dodo and the Eaglet are both sane and the Lory is mad.

♛ 24

THE KNAVE OF HEARTS I will prove that if Seven is mad, then Six must be sane—and therefore that the Knave was right in believing that Six, Seven are not both mad.

Well, suppose Seven is mad. Then Seven's belief about Five is wrong, so Five is sane. Then Five's belief is correct, so One and Four are either both mad or both sane. Now, it is not possible that One and Four are both mad. (Because if Four is mad, his belief is wrong, which makes Three and Two both mad, but Three's being mad means that One is sane rather than mad. Hence if Four is mad, One must be sane, so One and Four can't both be mad.) Therefore One and Four are both sane. Since Four is sane, then Three and Two are not both mad—at least one of them is sane. However, Three can't be sane, because he believes One is mad. Therefore it must be Two who is sane. Therefore One and Two are both sane. This means that Six's belief is correct, so Six must be sane.

We have therefore shown that if Seven is mad, then Six must be sane. Therefore it is not possible that Seven and Six are both mad. Since the Knave believes that they are not both mad, then the Knave must be sane.

### ♛ 25

THE GRYPHON'S EVALUATION   In Problem 15, we proved that the Cook is sane. So if the Duchess's story were correct, the Cook would be sane. But then the Duchess tells Alice that the Cook believes the Duchess to be mad. This would mean that the Duchess must be mad (because the Cook, who is sane, believes she is). Therefore, if the Duchess's entire story were true, she would have to be mad, which would mean that her story is not true. So if the story were true, we would have a contradiction. Therefore her story is not true.

Incidentally, the above argument is not intended to prove that the Duchess is mad; there is no reason to believe that she is. All it showed was that *if* her story were true, she would have to be mad, hence her story is not true. This means only that the Duchess is not correct in *all* her beliefs—not that she is *incorrect* in all her beliefs!

## Chapter 4

### ♛ 26

HOW MANY? However many tarts the Dormouse has, call that number *one portion*. So the Dormouse has one portion of tarts and the March Hare has twice as many tarts as the Dormouse (since the Dormouse has half as many as the March Hare), so the March Hare has two portions. The Hatter has three times as much as the March Hare, so the Hatter has six portions. Since the Hatter has six portions and the Dormouse has only one portion, then the Hatter has five portions more than the Dormouse. Also, the Hatter has twenty more tarts than the Dormouse, so five portions of tarts is the same as twenty tarts. This means that there are four tarts in one portion. So, the Dormouse has four tarts, the March Hare has eight, and the Hatter has twenty-four, which is indeed twenty more than the number the Dormouse has.

### ♛ 27

THE TABLES ARE TURNED! The March Hare took five-sixteenths of the tarts, which left eleven-sixteenths. Then the Dormouse took seven-elevenths of that—in other words, seven-elevenths of eleven-sixteenths. Well, $\frac{7}{11} \times \frac{11}{16} = \frac{7}{16}$, so the Dormouse took seven-sixteenths of all the tarts. Since the March Hare took five-sixteenths of all the tarts, the two together took seven-sixteenths and five-sixteenths, which is twelve-sixteenths. This left four-sixteenths, which is one-quarter of the tarts, for the Hatter. Also, eight tarts were left for the Hatter, so eight tarts is one-quarter of all the tarts. Therefore there were thirty-two tarts altogether. Now, one-sixteenth of thirty-two is two, so five-sixteenths of thirty-two is ten. Therefore the March Hare ate ten tarts. This left twenty-two tarts. Then the Dormouse ate seven-elevenths of the twenty-two remaining tarts, which is fourteen tarts (since one-eleventh of twenty-two is two, then seven-elevenths must be fourteen). This left eight tarts for the Hatter, so everything checks.

### ♛ 28

HOW MANY FAVORITES? This puzzle, usually solved by algebra, is extremely simple if looked at in the following way: Let us first give three tarts apiece to every one of the thirty guests. This leaves ten tarts. Now, all the nonfavorites have had all the tarts they are going to get, whereas each favorite is to get one more tart. So the ten remaining tarts are all for the favorites—one to each favorite. So there must be ten favorites.

Let us check: The ten favorites each get four tarts, which makes forty tarts. The other twenty guests each get three tarts apiece, which makes sixty tarts. Since forty plus sixty equals one hundred, we see our solution is correct.

### ♛ 29

LARGE TARTS AND SMALL TARTS Since each large tart is worth three small ones, then seven large tarts are worth twenty-one small ones, so seven large ones and four small ones are worth twenty-five small ones. On the other hand, four large ones and seven small ones are worth the same as nineteen small ones (because four large ones are worth twelve small ones). So the difference in price between twenty-five small ones and nineteen small ones is twelve cents. This means that six tarts (six is twenty-five minus nineteen) are worth twelve cents, so each small tart is worth two cents and each large tart is worth six cents.

Let us check: Four large tarts and seven small ones would cost 24 + 14 = 38 cents, whereas seven large tarts and four small ones would cost 42 + 8 = 50 cents, which is indeed 12 cents more than 38 cents.

### ♛ 30

THE VISIT The Cheshire Cat must have found two tarts, eaten half of them plus one, leaving none. The Dormouse must have found six tarts, eaten half of them plus one, leaving two for the Cheshire Cat. The March Hare found fourteen, ate seven plus one, leaving six. The Hatter found thirty, ate fifteen plus one, leaving fourteen. So there were thirty tarts to begin with.

### ♛ 31

HOW MANY DAYS DID HE WORK The maximum number of tarts the gardener can earn is 78 (3 × 26). He earned only 62 tarts, so he lost 16 tarts by his idleness. Now, each day he is idle means a loss of 4 tarts (the difference between being given 3 and having to give 1). Therefore he was idle 4 days and worked 22 days.

Let us check: For the 22 days he worked, he earned 66 tarts. For the 4 days he was idle, he had to give back 4 tarts, so he received only 62 tarts.

### ♛ 32

WHAT TIME WAS IT? A common wrong answer is six o'clock; the correct answer is five o'clock.

At five o'clock, the first chime of the Queen's clock coincided with the first chime of the King's clock. The second chime of the Queen's clock occurred at the same instant as the third chime of the King's clock. The third chime of the Queen's clock occurred at the fifth chime of the King's clock. The King's clock had then finished its chiming, and the Queen's clock had still two more chimes to go.

### ♛ 33

HOW MANY WERE LOST? Let us call the amount of food one man eats in one day—let us call this one portion. Then the 9 men originally had 45 portions of food (enough for 5 days), but on the second day they had only 36 portions left. Then they met the new party, and the 36 portions lasted all the men for 3 days. Therefore there must have been 12 men, so the new party consisted of 3 men.

### ♛ 34

HOW MUCH WATER WAS SPILLED? On the fifth day, before the water was spilled, there were eight days of water supply left. The spilled water would have served the man who died for eight days, so eight quarts were spilled.

### ♛ 35

WHEN WILL HE GET OUT OF PRISON? When the gaoler is twice the prisoner's age, the difference between their ages will be the prisoner's age. Also, the difference between their ages will be the same as it is now—namely 29 years. So when the prisoner is 29, the gaoler will be twice as old (58). So the prisoner has to wait 4 years.

## ♛ 36

HOW LONG TO GET OUT? The answer is not 30 days; the frog could get out on the evening of the 28th day. On the morning of the 2nd day, the frog will be one foot from the bottom; on the morning of the 3rd day he will be 2 feet from the bottom—and so forth until the morning of the 28th day, when he will be 27 feet from the bottom. On the evening of that day he will have reached the top, and so will not have to slide back again.

## ♛ 37

DID HE CATCH THE TRAIN? The cyclist made the mistake of averaging over distances rather than times! If he had spent equal times going four miles an hour, eight miles an hour, and twelve miles an hour, he would indeed have averaged eight miles an hour, but he spent most of his time going uphill and least of his time going downhill.

It is easy to calculate how long the trip took him: He spent one hour going uphill, a half-hour—or thirty minutes—going on level ground, and one-third of an hour—or twenty minutes—going downhill. This adds up to an hour and fifty minutes, so he missed the train by twenty minutes.

## ♛ 38

WHAT ABOUT THIS ONE? When the man arrived at the first station, the train had left a minute earlier. Ten miles an hour is one mile in 6 minutes, or 1½ miles in 9 minutes. So the train reached the second station 8 minutes after the man arrived at the first station. The train waits 14½ minutes at the second station, so the man has 22½ minutes to catch the train at the second station. Four miles an hour is one mile in 15 minutes, or 1½ miles in 22½ minutes, so the man just caught the train.

### ♛39

HOW FAR AWAY IS THE SCHOOL? The difference between being 5 minutes late and being 10 minutes early is a difference of 15 minutes. So the boy will save 15 minutes if he walks at the rate of 5 miles an hour rather than 4 miles an hour. Now, 5 miles an hour is one mile in 12 minutes, and 4 miles an hour is one mile in 15 minutes, so walking at the faster rate, he saves 3 minutes in every mile, which is 15 minutes in 5 miles. So the school is 5 miles away.

Let us check: If he walks at 5 miles an hour, he will take one hour. If he walks at 4 miles an hour, he will take 1¼ hours (one hour for the first 4 miles and a quarter of an hour for the last mile)—which is one hour and 15 minutes. So there is indeed a 15-minute difference.

### ♛40

IS THIS PUZZLE SAD? Yes, it is a bit sad, in a way, because the dealer miscalculated: He didn't break even; he lost $20 that day.

Let us see why: Consider first the painting he sold at a 10 percent profit. He got $990 for the painting; how much did he pay for it? Now the profit is not 10 percent of $990, but 10 percent of the amount he paid. So $990 is 110 percent—or $11/10$—of what he paid. This means he paid $10/11$ of $990, which is $900. This checks, because he paid $900, made 10 percent of $900, which is $90, so he received $990. Therefore he made $90 on the first painting.

Now let us consider the second painting: He lost 10 percent of what he paid for it, so he sold it for 90 percent—which is $9/10$—of what he paid. Therefore he paid $10/9$ of $990, which is $1,100. Does this check? Yes, because he paid $1,100, and 10 percent of $1,100 is $110, so he sold it for $1,100 minus $110, which is $990.

So he lost $110 on the second painting, and gained only $90 on the first one, so his net loss was $20.

♛ 41

WHO IS OLDER? We must first determine how many days it will take for the two watches to be together again. Since the March Hare's watch loses time at the same rate as the Hatter's watch gains, then the next time the watches will be together again is when the Hatter's watch has gained six hours and the March Hare's watch has lost six hours. (Then both watches will read six o'clock, and, of course, both watches will be wrong.) Now, how many days will it take for the Hatter's watch to gain six hours? Well, a gain of 10 seconds an hour is one minute in six hours, which is 4 minutes a day, which is one hour in 15 days, which is 6 hours in 90 days. So in 90 days the watches will be together again.

Now, we were not told on what day in January the two watches were set right. If it were any day other than January 1, 90 days later couldn't possibly fall in March; it would have to fall in April (or possibly May). So the watches must have been set right on January 1. But even then, 90 days later couldn't fall on any day in March unless it's leap year! (The reader can check this with a calendar. Ninety days after January 1 is April 1 on an ordinary year, and March 31 on a leap year.) This proves that the March Hare's twenty-first birthday falls in a leap year, hence he must have been born in 1843, rather than 1842 or 1844. (Twenty-one years after 1843 is 1864, which is a leap year.) We are given that one of the two was born in 1842, hence it was the Hatter who was born in 1842. So the Hatter is older than the March Hare.

## Chapter 5

♛ 42

ENTER THE FIRST SPY   C certainly cannot be a knight, because no knight would lie and claim to be the spy. Therefore, C is either a knave or the spy. Suppose C were the spy. Then A's claim is false, which makes A a knave (he can't be the spy, because C is). This leaves B as the knight, but then how could he, a knight, make the false claim that A is a knight? So it is impossible that C is the spy. Therefore, C is the knave. Then B's claim is false, which means he is a knave or the spy, but C is the knave, so B must be the spy. This leaves A as the knight. So A is the knight, B is the spy, and C is the knave.

### ♛ 43

THE CASE OF THE BUNGLING SPY   One false statement which would convict him is "I am a knave." A knight could never lie and claim to be a knave, and a knave would not tell the truth and say he is a knave. Only the spy could claim to be a knave.

### ♛ 44

ANOTHER BUNGLING SPY   A true statement which would convict him is "I am not a knight." Again, neither a knight nor a knave could say that, because a knight would not lie and say that he is not a knight, and a knave would not tell the truth and say that he is not a knight. So only the spy could say that.

### ♛ 45

THE CASE OF THE FOXY SPY If A had answered yes, he would have got convicted, because the court would have reasoned as follows:

"Suppose B were the spy. Then all three are telling the truth, which is impossible, since one of them is a knave. Therefore, B can't be the spy. His statement, therefore, was false, so B is the knave. C's statement was false, and since C is not the knave, he is the spy."

So, if C had answered yes, the court would have known that he is the spy. Therefore, C cleverly answered no, and the court could not tell whether or not he was the spy. (As far as the court could know, either he could be a knight and B the spy, or a knave and A the spy, or he could be the spy.)

### ☙46

WHO IS MURDOCH? Since A claims to be the spy, then he is either a knave or the spy. Likewise C claims to be the spy, so he also is either a knave or the spy. So one of A, C is a knave and the other a spy. Therefore, B is the knight; hence his statement is true; so A must be the spy.

### ☙47

THE RETURN OF MURDOCH If A is Murdoch, all three statements are true, which is impossible since one of them is a knave. If C is Murdoch, all three statements are false, which is also impossible since one of the three is a knight. Therefore, B must be Murdoch.

### ☙48

A MORE INTERESTING CASE If we had not been told that after C's accusation the judge knew who the spy was, then we could not solve this problem. But we *are* given that the judge knew, and this is the vital clue!

Suppose C had accused A. Then the judge couldn't have known who was the spy, because it could be that A is the spy, B the knave, and C the knight, or that B is the spy, A the knight, and C the knave, or it could also be that C is the spy, A the knave, and B the knight. So if C had accused A, the judge couldn't have made a conviction.

Now, let's see what happens if C accused B. This means that A and C both accused B. Then their accusations are either both true or both false. If they were both true, then B would really be the spy, and since the accusations are true, A and C must both be knights (neither could be a spy, since B is), and it is not possible that there are two knights. Therefore, their accusations were false, which means that B is not the spy. Could A be the spy? No, for it he were, then B and C would have both lied in accusing each other, which would make both of them knaves, which is not possible. Therefore, the only possibility is that C is the spy (and B, having accused C, is the knight, and A, having accused B, is the knave).

In summary, if C accused A, then the judge couldn't have made a conviction, but if C accused B, the judge would know that C was the spy. Since the judge *did* know, then it must have been that C accused B, and the judge then convicted C.

### ♛49

A STILL MORE INTERESTING CASE   We do not know what A and B answered. There are four possible cases to consider: (1) A, B both said yes; (2) A said no and B said yes; (3) A said yes and B said no; (4) both said no.

These cases will come up again in the next two problems, and we will now analyze them with care.

*Case 1—they both said yes:* Since A claims he is the spy, then he is either the knave or the spy (because a knight could never claim to be a spy). If A is the knave, then he lied; hence B lied when he said that A told the truth; so B is not a knight, and since A is the knave, B is the spy. This means that C must be the knight. So if A is the knave, B is the spy, and C is the knight.

Suppose A is the spy. Then he answered truthfully; so B answered truthfully in saying that A answered truthfully; so B must be the knight. This makes C the knave. So if A is the spy, then B is the knight, and C is the knave. Let us record these two possibilities (which we'll call 1a and 1b) of Case 1:

|     | A     | B      | C      |
|-----|-------|--------|--------|
| 1a  | KNAVE | SPY    | KNIGHT |
| 1b  | SPY   | KNIGHT | KNAVE  |

*Case 2—A said no and B said yes:* Since A denied being the spy, he is the knight or the spy. (A knave would lie and say he was the spy.) If A is the knight, he told the truth; hence B also told the truth in affirming that A told the truth; so B can't be the knave, so he must be the spy. This makes C the knave.

If A is the spy, then he lied; hence B also lied when he affirmed that A told the truth, which makes B the knave; hence C must be the knight. So here are the two possibilities—2a and 2b—under Case 2:

|     | A      | B     | C      |
|-----|--------|-------|--------|
| 2a  | KNIGHT | SPY   | KNAVE  |
| 2b  | SPY    | KNAVE | KNIGHT |

*Case 3—A said yes and B said no:* Since A claims to be the spy, then (as in Case 1) A must be the knave or the spy. If he is the knave, then he lied; so B told the truth; hence either B is the knight (and C the spy) or B is the spy (and C is the knight). If A is the spy, then he told the truth; hence B lied, which means B is the knave and C the knight. Thus we have three possibilities:

|     | A     | B      | C      |
|-----|-------|--------|--------|
| 3a  | KNAVE | KNIGHT | SPY    |
| 3b  | KNAVE | SPY    | KNIGHT |
| 3c  | SPY   | KNAVE  | KNIGHT |

*Case 4—both said no:* Since A denied being the spy, then (like Case 2) he is the knight or the spy. Suppose he is the knight. Then he told the truth. Then B lied; so either he is the knave (and C the spy), or he is the spy (and C the knave). Suppose A is the spy. Then he told the truth; hence B also told the truth, which means B is the knight (and C is the knave). So we again have three possibilities:

|     | A      | B      | C     |
|-----|--------|--------|-------|
| 4a  | KNIGHT | KNAVE  | SPY   |
| 4b  | KNIGHT | SPY    | KNAVE |
| 4c  | SPY    | KNIGHT | KNAVE |

For convenient reference, let us record all four cases in the following table.

TABLE I

*Case 1—Both said yes*

|  | A | B | C |
|---|---|---|---|
| 1a | KNAVE | SPY | KNIGHT |
| 1b | SPY | KNIGHT | KNAVE |

*Case 2—A said no and B said yes*

|  | A | B | C |
|---|---|---|---|
| 2a | KNIGHT | SPY | KNAVE |
| 2b | SPY | KNAVE | KNIGHT |

*Case 3—A said yes and B said no*

|  | A | B | C |
|---|---|---|---|
| 3a | KNAVE | KNIGHT | SPY |
| 3b | KNAVE | SPY | KNIGHT |
| 3c | SPY | KNAVE | KNIGHT |

*Case 4—Both said no*

|  | A | B | C |
|---|---|---|---|
| 4a | KNIGHT | KNAVE | SPY |
| 4b | KNIGHT | SPY | KNAVE |
| 4c | SPY | KNIGHT | KNAVE |

Now, we are given that after A and B answered the judge's questions, the judge knew that C was not the spy. If Case 3 were the one that occurred, then the judge couldn't know whether C was a spy or a knight. If Case 4 occurred, the judge couldn't know whether C was a spy or a knave. But the judge *did* know that C wasn't the spy. Therefore, Case 3 and Case 4 are ruled out; so it was either Case 1 or Case 2.

Now, the judge knows that A spoke the truth when he said that C is not a spy; so he knows that A must be either the knight or the spy. If Case 2 held, the judge couldn't have known whether A was the knight or the spy; hence he couldn't have known who the spy was. So Case 1 holds, and the judge knew that A can't be a knave (since he made a true statement); hence A must be the spy.

**꙼ 50**

AN EQUALLY INTERESTING CASE   Since A, B were asked the same questions as in the last problem, we can use the same table (see page 161).

Consider that point of the trial right before the judge asked C whether he was a spy. At that point, the judge did not know of any of the three that he was definitely not the spy; otherwise he would have acquitted him. This rules out Cases 1 and 2, because in either of those cases the judge would have known that C was either a knight or a knave and would have acquitted him. So either Case 3 or Case 4 must hold.

Now, we consider the judge's reasoning after C answered. Suppose Case 3 holds. Then the judge knows that C is either the spy or the knight. If C answered no, the judge would have known no more than before and couldn't have convicted anyone. If C answered yes, the judge would have known that C was the spy, because a knight could not say that he was the spy. So, if Case 3 holds, then it must have been C who was convicted.

Suppose Case 4 holds. Then the judge knows that C is the spy or the knave. If C answered yes, the judge couldn't have made a conviction (because either a knave or a spy could say he is a spy). If C answered no, then the judge would have known that C was the spy, because a knave could not make the true statement that he isn't a spy. So in Case 4, it was also C who was convicted.

It might be well to point out that it is impossible for you or me to know whether Case 3 or Case 4 is the one which actually holds, nor is it possible for us to know what answer C actually gave. All we do know is that since the judge did make a conviction, then either Case 3 holds and C answered yes, or Case 4 holds and C answered no, and that C was convicted in either case. So we know that C was the spy.

### ♛ 51

THE MOST INTERESTING CASE OF ALL    We use the same table that we used in the solution to the last two problems (the table is on page 161).

*Step 1:* After B answered the judge's question, the judge made an acquittal. If either Case 3 or Case 4 held, then any of the three defendants could have been the spy, and the judge could not have made an acquittal. Therefore, Case 1 or Case 2 must be the one that holds, and in both cases, C cannot be the spy, but either of the others could be. So it was C who was acquitted. So we know that C was acquitted and that either Case 1 or Case 2 holds, and we can now completely forget about Cases 3 and 4.

After C left the court, the judge asked either A or B (we don't know which) whether the other was a spy, and he got the answer Yes or No, but again we don't know which. Thus there are four possibilities for Case 1 and four possibilities for Case 2, making eight possibilities altogether. Now we shall eliminate half of them, using the given fact that the judge, after getting the answer, made a conviction.

Suppose Case 1 holds. Suppose A were the one who was asked the question. If he answered yes (thus claiming that B was the spy), the judge could have eliminated 1a, because if A is a knave and B the spy, A could not have told the truth that B is the spy. Thus the judge would have eliminated 1a and known that 1b must hold and that A is the spy. If A answered no, the judge could not have made a conviction, because it could be that A is a knave who lied when he said that B wasn't the spy, or A could be the spy who told the truth when he said that B wasn't the spy. Therefore, it is not the case that A answered no. So if A was the one who was asked, then he answered yes and was convicted. Now, suppose it was B who was asked whether A was the spy. If B answered yes, then the judge couldn't have made a conviction (as the reader can see by examining both possibilities 1a and 1b and seeing that B could answer no in either case), but if B answered no, the judge would know that B must be the spy (because 1b is ruled out, since it would mean that B, a knight, denied that A [a spy] is a spy). So B must have answered no, and B was then convicted. This completes our analysis of Case 1.

Case 2 can be analyzed in a similar manner, and we rely on the reader to fill in details. Suppose Case 2 holds. If A was the one questioned, then he must have answered no for the judge to have been enabled to make a conviction, and A was convicted. If B was the one questioned, he must have answered yes for the judge to have been enabled to make a conviction, and B was convicted. We leave the verification of these facts to the reader (which, as I have said, is not very different from the reasoning of Case 1).

Let us summarize what we know so far:

If Case 1 holds, then either A was asked the third question, answered yes, and was the spy, or B was asked the third question, answered no, and was the spy.

If Case 2 holds, then either A was asked the third question, answered no, and was the spy, or B was asked the third question, answered yes, and was the spy.

We thus have the following four possibilities:

| CASE | THE THREE ANSWERS | | | SPY |
|------|-----|-----|-----|-----|
|      | 1st | 2nd | 3rd |     |
| 1a   | Yes | Yes | Yes | A   |
| 1b   | Yes | Yes | No  | B   |
| 2a   | No  | Yes | No  | A   |
| 2b   | No  | Yes | Yes | B   |

*Step 2:* This is as far as we can get without the additional information about the two friends of Mr. Anthony. We are given that either both of them solved the case, or that neither of them did; we will prove that it is impossible that both of them solved the problem.

Consider the first friend: If Mr. Anthony answered him affirmatively, then the friend would have known that Case 1a must hold and that A is the spy; if Mr. Anthony answered negatively, then the friend would have been unable to know which of Cases 1b, 2a, 2b held, and could not have known whether A or B was the spy. So the only way that the first friend could have solved the problem is that Mr. Anthony answered affirmatively and that Case 1a holds.

As to the second friend, if Mr. Anthony answered him affirmatively, then this friend would have known that Case 2a must hold and that A is the spy, but if Mr. Anthony answered him negatively, then the second friend couldn't have solved the problem. And so the only way the second friend could have solved the problem is that Case 2a holds and that Mr. Anthony answered him affirmatively. Now it cannot be that Case 1a and Case 2a both hold, and therefore Mr. Anthony could not have given an affirmative answer to both his friends, and so it is impossible that both friends were able to solve the problem. Therefore neither friend solved the problem (since we are given that either both did or neither did), and so Mr. Anthony did not answer either question affirmatively. This rules out Case 1a and Case 2a, so B must be the spy.

## Chapter 6

♛ 52

THE FIRST QUESTION Alice made the mistake of writing eleven thousand eleven hundred and eleven as 11,111—which is wrong! 11,111 is eleven thousand, *one* hundred and eleven! To see the correct way of writing eleven thousand eleven hundred and eleven, add them up like this:

$$
\begin{array}{r}
11{,}000 \\
1{,}100 \\
\underline{11} \\
12{,}111
\end{array}
$$

So, eleven thousand eleven hundred and eleven is 12,111—which is exactly divisible by 3.

♛ 53

ANOTHER DIVISION A million *multiplied* by a quarter is a quarter of a million, but a million *divided* by a quarter is the number of quarters needed to make a million, which is four million. So, four million is the correct answer to the Queen's question.

♛ 54

HOW MUCH? A common wrong answer is "Four shillings." If the bottle was really worth 4 shillings, then the wine, being worth 26 shillings more, would be worth 30 shillings; so the bottle and wine together would be worth 34 shillings.

The correct answer is that the bottle is worth 2 shillings and the wine is worth 28 shillings.

♛ 55

AWAKE OR ASLEEP? If the Red King were awake at the time, he could not have had the false belief that both he and the Red Queen were asleep. Therefore, he was asleep. This means that his belief was false, so it is not true that both were asleep. Therefore, the Red Queen was awake.

♛ 56

AWAKE OR ASLEEP? The Red King was either awake or asleep at the time. Suppose he were awake. Then his belief was correct, which means the Red Queen was asleep. Then her belief was incorrect, so she believed he was asleep. On the other hand, suppose he were asleep at the time. Then his belief was wrong, so the Red Queen was awake. Then her belief was correct, so she believed he was asleep. Therefore, regardless of whether the King was awake or asleep, the Queen must have believed he was asleep.

♛ 57

HOW MANY RATTLES? If Tweedledum loses, he will have half the total number of rattles (which is the same thing as having the same number as Tweedledee), so he now has one more than half the total. If he wins the bet, then he will have two more than half the total. Also, he will then have two-thirds of the total (which is the same thing as having twice as many as Tweedledee), which is one-sixth of the total more than half the total (because the difference between one-half and one-third is one-sixth). Therefore, one-sixth of the total more than half the total is the same thing as two more than half the total, so two rattles is the same thing as half the total. Therefore, the total number of rattles is twelve, so Tweedledum has seven and Tweedledee has five.

Let us check: If Tweedledum loses, each will have six; if Tweedledum wins, he will have eight and Tweedledee will have four, so he will have twice as many as Tweedledee.

### ♛58

HOW MANY BROTHERS AND SISTERS? There are four boys and three girls in the family. Tony has three brothers and three sisters; Alice has four brothers and two sisters.

### ♛59

HOW MANY WERE WRONG? Exactly three right is the same thing as exactly one wrong, so the choice is between exactly three right and exactly two right. Now, it is impossible to get exactly three right, because if three are right, the fourth must also be right! Therefore, she got exactly two right.

### ♛60

HOW MUCH LAND? A common wrong answer is 11 acres. If there had really been 11 acres, the tax collector would have taken away 1$\frac{1}{10}$ acres (which is one-tenth of 11 acres), which would have left the farmer with 9$\frac{9}{10}$ acres rather than 10 acres, so 11 acres cannot be the right answer.

How does one find the right answer? Well, look at it this way: After one-tenth of the farmer's land had been taken away, he had nine-tenths left. So $\frac{9}{10}$ of the original piece is 10 acres. This means that if we multiply the number of acres in the original piece by $\frac{9}{10}$, we get the present piece—10 acres. So, to get from the present piece back to the original piece, we must *divide* by $\frac{9}{10}$! Now, to divide by $\frac{9}{10}$ is to multiply by $\frac{10}{9}$, so we multiply 10 by $\frac{10}{9}$, getting $\frac{100}{9}$, which is $11\frac{1}{9}$ acres.

Does this check? Let us see: The original piece is $11\frac{1}{9}$ acres. One-tenth of $11\frac{1}{9}$ is $1\frac{1}{9}$, so taking that away leaves exactly 10 acres.


♛61

ANOTHER ACREAGE PROBLEM Reducing everything to six-tieths, $\frac{1}{3} + \frac{1}{4} + \frac{1}{5} = \frac{20}{60} + \frac{15}{60} + \frac{12}{60} = \frac{47}{60}$. This leaves $\frac{13}{60}$ for the cultivation of corn. Therefore, $\frac{13}{60}$ of the land is 26 acres, and since 13 is half of 26, then 60 must be half of the total number of acres. So the land has 120 acres.

Let us check: One-third of 120 is 40, which is for the squash; one-fourth of 120 is 30, which is for the peas; and one-fifth of 120 is 24, which is for the beans. Now $40 + 30 + 24 = 94$, which leaves 26 acres for the corn.


♛62

THE CLOCK STRIKES TWELVE Between the first stroke and the sixth stroke there are five intervals of time, and it takes thirty seconds to cover those five intervals; so the interval between any two consecutive strokes is six seconds (not five seconds, as some people mistakenly conclude!). Now, between the first stroke and the twelfth, there are eleven time intervals; so it takes the clock sixty-six seconds.


♛63

THE TWELFTH QUESTION Suppose Alice had answered yes. Then the Queen could fail her or pass her, as she pleased. If she failed her, and Alice asked why, the Queen could say, "You got the last question wrong—after all, you said you would pass and you didn't—and since you got the last question wrong, you have to fail!"

On the other hand, the Queen could equally as well have passed her and said, "You predicted you would pass, and since you passed, you predicted correctly; so you answered the last question right, and that's why you pass. (Of course, both reasonings are circular, but neither one is any worse than the other!)

On the other hand, if Alice answered no, then the Queen could neither pass her nor fail her. If the Queen passed her, then Alice did not predict correctly, and having given the wrong answer, by all rights she should have failed! If the Queen failed her, then Alice predicted correctly, and having given the right answer, she should have passed! So the Queen could neither pass her nor fail her.

As I said, Alice was more interested in not failing than in passing; hence she answered, "No," and this, indeed, completely stymied the Queen.

## Chapter 7

### ♛ 64

ROUND ONE   If the speaker were telling the truth, then he would be Tweedledum and he would be carrying a black card, but he cannot be speaking the truth and also carry a black card. Therefore, he must be lying. This means that his card really is black, and since his statement was false, he is not really Tweedledum carrying a black card; so he is Tweedledee carrying a black card.

### ♛ 65

ROUND TWO   The speaker asserts that he is not Tweedledum carrying a red card. His assertion must be true, for if he *were* Tweedledum carrying a red card, then, since his card is red, he couldn't lie and say that he is *not* Tweedledum carrying a red card. So it is true that he is not Tweedledum carrying a red card. Since his statement is true, then he must in fact be carrying a red card. But since his statement is true, he is not Tweedledum carrying a red card; so he must be Tweedledee carrying a red card.

### ♛66

ROUND THREE   *Either-or* means *at least one* (and possibly both); so if he were carrying a black card, then it would be true that *either* he is Tweedledum *or* he is carrying a black card, which would mean that a holder of a black card made a true statement. This is impossible, so his card cannot be black. Since his card is red, his statement is true, which means that *either* he is Tweedledum *or* his card is black. Since the second alternative doesn't hold, then he must be Tweedledum. So he is Tweedledum carrying a red card.

### ♛67

ROUND FOUR   This time it cannot be determined whether he is holding a red or a black card, but in either case, he must be Tweedledee. Suppose his card is red. Then he speaks truly, so he is either Tweedledum carrying a black card, or Tweedledee carrying a red card. He can't be the former (since his card is red), hence he must be the latter, so he is Tweedledee.

On the other hand, suppose his card is black. Then his statement is false, which means that he is neither Tweedledum with black nor Tweedledee with red. So he is either Tweedledum with red or Tweedledee with black. The former is not possible (since his card is black), so the latter holds—which means again that he is Tweedledee.

### 68

ROUND FIVE   Suppose the speaker is carrying a red card. Then his statement is true, whih means that Tweedledum is carrying a black card; so the speaker must be Tweedledee. Suppose the speaker is carrying a black card. Then his statement is false; so Tweedledum is not carrying a black card. Yet the speaker is carrying a black card; so he can't be Tweedledum—again he must be Tweedledee. So in either case, the speaker is Tweedledee.

### ♛ 69

ROUND SIX  If the first one were holding a red card, we would get the following contradiction: Suppose the first one were red. Then his statement is true; hence his brother is Tweedledee, so he is Tweedledum. Thus he is Tweedledum carrying a red card. This makes the second one's statement true. But then, how could the first one, who is truthful, lie and say that his brother is Tweedledee holding a *black* card? So it is impossible that the first one is carrying red; he must be carrying a black card.

Since the first one is not red, then the second one's statement cannot be true; so the second one is also carrying a black card. If the second one were Tweedledee, then he would be Tweedledee carrying a black card, which would make the first one's statement true. But the first one's statement is false (because the first one is carrying a black card); so the second one can't be Tweedledee. This proves that the first one must be Tweedledee.

### ♛ 70

ROUND ONE (ORANGE AND PURPLE)  The speaker couldn't have been Tweedledum carrying an orange card, or he would have told the truth and said, "My card is orange." The speaker couldn't have been Tweedledum carrying a purple card, or he would have lied and said, "My card is orange." Therefore, the speaker was not Tweedledum; so it was Tweedledee (who either carried a purple card and told the truth, or an orange card and lied).

### ♛ 71

ROUND TWO (ORANGE AND PURPLE)  A useful principle, which will be used in this problem and some of the later ones, is this: If the two cards are of the same color, then one of them is lying and the other is telling the truth (because if they are both orange, Tweedledum is telling the truth and Tweedledee is lying; if they are both purple, then Tweedledee is telling the truth and Tweedledum is lying). On the other hand, if the cards are of different colors, then the brothers are either both lying or both telling the truth.

Now, let us consider the present problem. Since both brothers claim to be Tweedledum, then clearly one is lying and one is telling the truth. Therefore, both cards must be of the same color. Suppose they were both purple. Then the first one's second statement is false; hence his first statement is false; hence he is Tweedledee, which would mean that Tweedledee with a purple card is lying, which is not possible. Therefore, both cards are orange. Hence the first one's second statement is true, which means that his first statement is also true, so he is Tweedledum. So, the first one is Tweedledum, the second is Tweedledee, and both are carrying orange cards.

### ♛72

ROUND THREE (ORANGE AND PURPLE) Looking at the first two statements, we can tell they are obviously either both true or both false. Therefore, their cards are of different colors (see the principle discussed at the beginning of the last solution). So the first one lied when he said that the cards are of the same color. So the first one also lied when he said he was Tweedledee. So he is Tweedledum.

### ♛73

ROUND FOUR (ORANGE AND PURPLE) Since the two make contradictory claims, then one is lying and one is telling the truth. Therefore, their cards are of the same color (same principle!). If the cards are both purple, then the first one is telling the truth; so he must be Tweedledee (because his card is purple and he is telling the truth). If both cards are orange, then the first one is lying, hence again must be Tweedledee (because his card is orange and he is lying). So in either case, the first one is Tweedledee.

♛74

ROUND FIVE (ORANGE AND PURPLE) The first statement of the first one agrees with the statement of the second one, so they are either both lying or both telling the truth. Therefore, their cards are of different colors (same principle again!). This means that it is true that at least one card is purple; so the first one is telling the truth. Therefore, his second statement is also true, so he is Tweedledum. (Also, his card is orange and Tweedledee's is purple.)

♛75

ROUND SIX (ORANGE AND PURPLE) The two are contradicting each other, so one is lying and one is telling the truth. Therefore, their cards are of the same color (same principle again!). This means the first one's statement is true.

♛76

WHO IS WHO? The figure on the back is either a square or a circle. Suppose it is a square. Then a square means yes and a circle means no, so the second brother's answer meant no, which was a lie! On the other hand, suppose the figure on the back is a circle. Then a circle means yes, so the second brother's answer meant yes, which is again a lie, since a square was *not* on the back! Therefore, the second brother lied, so he is Tweedledee.

♛77

WHAT QUESTION SHOULD ALICE ASK? Many questions can be devised which will do this; the simplest one I can think of is "Is your card red?"

Whatever sign is given in answer must mean yes, because one with a red card would truthfully say it is red, and one with a black card would lie and claim his card is red. So the second one's response meant yes. Suppose he responded by drawing a square in the air. Then he means yes by a square; hence he has the prize. If he responded by drawing a circle, then he means yes by a circle and no by a square, so he doesn't have the prize.

In summary, if he draws a square, he has the prize; if he draws a circle, then the other one has the prize.


## Chapter 9

In all the solutions for this chapter we shall let A be the first defendant, B the second defendant, and C the third defendant.


### ☞78

WHICH ONE WAS GUILTY? We are given that the guilty one lied. If B were guilty, he would have told the truth when he accused himself; therefore, B cannot be guilty. If A were guilty, then all three of them would have lied (because A would have accused either B or C, both of whom were innocent; B would have accused himself, who was innocent; and C would have accused either C, who was innocent, or A, who is innocent). But we are given that not all of them lied, so A can't be guilty either. So C was guilty.


### ☞79

THE SECOND ACCOUNT What could the White King have been told which enabled him to know who the guilty one was? If he had been told that all three of them lied, he could never have known who was guilty, because it could be that A was guilty and accused B, and B and C accused each other (so all of them lied); or it could be that B was guilty and accused C, and A and C accused each other (again all of them lied); or again it could be C was guilty and accused A, and A and B accused each other. So the White King was not told that all of them lied.

Could the King have solved the case if he had been told that exactly two of them lied, and which two they were? No: Suppose, for example, he was told that A told the truth and that B and C both lied. Then whoever A accused was guilty (since A told the truth), so he might have accused B (in which case B was guilty) and B and C both lied and accused A (or maybe B accused C, and C accused A). On the other hand, it could be that A accused C and that B and C both accused A, in which case C was guilty. So if A was the only one who told the truth, then either B or C could be guilty. Similarly, if B was the only one who told the truth, then either A or C could be guilty, and if C was the only one who told the truth, then either A or B could be guilty. So if the White King had been told either that A was the only one who told the truth, or that B was, or that C was, he could never have known who was guilty. So he was not told any of these three things.

Could he have been told that all three told the truth? No, this is impossible, because the guilty one certainly lied (since he accused one of the others, and both the others were innocent).

This leaves only the case that exactly one lied. Well, if exactly one lied, then the one who lied must be the guilty one, because if an innocent one lied, that would make two lies—his and the guilty one's. So, therefore, the White King was told one of three things:

*Case 1:* A lied, B told the truth, C told the truth.

*Case 2:* A told the truth, B lied, C told the truth.

*Case 3:* A told the truth, B told the truth, C lied.

We now see how the White King knew who was guilty, but how can *we* know, since we don't know which of the three cases the King was told? Well, Humpty Dumpty either asked the White Knight whether any two consecutive statements were false, or he asked whether any two consecutive statements were true. The first question would have been a pointless one (since there is only one false statement), and had he asked it, the answer would have been no, and this wouldn't have enabled Humpty Dumpty to know which of the three cases held. So Humpty Dumpty asked whether any two consecutive statements were true. Had he been told "Yes," he would have ruled out Case 2, but couldn't have known who was guilty. But Humpty Dumpty *did* know, so he must have gotten No for an answer and then realized that Case 2 must be the one; so B is guilty.

♛ 80

THE NEXT TRIAL   This problem is quite simple: Since A told the truth and accused one of the others, then B or C must be guilty. Therefore A is innocent. If everyone changed his accusation, but still accused someone else, B would have told the truth, and since we know that A is innocent, B would have accused C. Therefore C is guilty.

♛ 81

THE NEXT TRIAL   Since A told the truth, and he accused either B or C, then either B or C is guilty; so A is innocent.

Now, the White Knight was either told that C lied or that C told the truth. If he had been told that C lied, he could not have known who was guilty, because it could be that C is guilty and falsely accused A (or for that matter B), or it could be that B is guilty and C falsely accused A. So, given that C lied, there is no way to determine whether B or C is guilty. On the other hand, given that C told the truth, he couldn't have accused A (who is innocent), so he accused B, and since he told the truth, B must be guilty. Therefore, the Jabberwocky must have told the White Knight that C told the truth, and the White Knight then knew that B must be guilty.

♛ 82

ANOTHER CASE   Again, since A told the truth and accused one of the others, he must be innocent. Now, if the White Knight had been told that C told the truth, then, without further information, he would have known that B was guilty (as we have seen in the solution of the last problem). But the White Knight could not, without further information, tell who was guilty; therefore, he must have been told that C lied. Then he was told whom C accused, and this enabled him to know who was guilty. If he had been told that C accused A, he couldn't have known whether B or C was guilty. So he must have been told that C accused B, which means that B must be innocent (since C lied), and since A is also innocent, C must be guilty.

♛ 83

ANOTHER CASE   There are eight possible cases for what A, B, C could have said. There are two possibilities for what A said, and with each of these two possibilities there are two possibilities for B; thus there are four possibilities for what A, B said. (These possibilities are [1] A, B both claimed to be guilty; [2] A said he was guilty; B said he was innocent; [3] A said he was innocent; B said he was guilty; [4] A, B both claimed to be innocent.) Now, with each of these four possibilities for A and B, there are two possibilities for what C said, so there are eight possibilities altogether for what A, B, C said.

With each of these eight possible cases for what the defendants said, there are three possibilities for which of the three defendants was actually guilty. Therefore, there are twenty-four possibilities for the whole business (the whole business being what each defendant said together with which one was actually guilty). If we knew which of these twenty-four possibilities held, we would of course know which one lied and which ones told the truth. We will now make a systematic table for each of these twenty-four possibilities. This table will be used not only for this puzzle but for a later one as well. Explanations immediately follow the table.

The *L*'s and *T*'s indicate who was lying and who was telling the truth (*L* stands for *lying* and *T* for *truth-telling*). For example, in Case 5B (which we find in Group 5 under the B column) we see that A was lying, B was lying, and C was telling the truth. (Case 5B means, of course, the case in which A said he was guilty, B said he was innocent, and C said A was innocent, and B was actually guilty.) More examples: In Case 8C, all three were lying; in Case 3B, all three were telling the truth; in Case 4C, A was telling the truth and B, C were both lying.

Now, the Jabberwocky, after being told what each defendant said, and also that there was at least one true statement and at least one false statement, knew who was guilty. What could the Jabberwocky have been told to have enabled him to know? Suppose he were told that A claimed innocence, B claimed innocence, and C claimed A was innocent (this takes us within the three possibilities of Case 1). The Jabberwocky could then have ruled out that C was guilty

| CASE | WHAT THEY SAID | A GUILTY | B GUILTY | C GUILTY |
|------|----------------|----------|----------|----------|
| 1 | A—I am innocent<br>B—I am innocent<br>C—A is innocent | L<br>T<br>L | T<br>L<br>T | T<br>T<br>T |
| 2 | A—I am innocent<br>B—I am innocent<br>C—A is guilty | L<br>T<br>T | T<br>L<br>L | T<br>T<br>T |
| 3 | A—I am innocent<br>B—I am guilty<br>C—A is innocent | L<br>L<br>L | T<br>T<br>T | T<br>L<br>T |
| 4 | A—I am innocent<br>B—I am guilty<br>C—A is guilty | L<br>L<br>T | T<br>T<br>L | T<br>L<br>L |
| 5 | A—I am guilty<br>B—I am innocent<br>C—A is innocent | T<br>T<br>L | L<br>L<br>T | L<br>T<br>T |
| 6 | A—I am guilty<br>B—I am innocent<br>C—A is guilty | T<br>T<br>T | L<br>L<br>L | L<br>T<br>L |
| 7 | A—I am guilty<br>B—I am guilty<br>C—A is innocent | T<br>L<br>L | L<br>T<br>T | L<br>L<br>T |
| 8 | A—I am guilty<br>B—I am guilty<br>C—A is guilty | T<br>L<br>T | L<br>T<br>L | L<br>L<br>L |

(because in Case 1C all three lied), but he could not possibly tell whether A or B was guilty (because in Case 1A there is at least one true and at least one false statement, and likewise with Case 1B). Therefore, the Jabberwocky was *not* told this (because he *did* know who was guilty). What about Case 2—A claimed to be innocent, B claimed to be innocent, and C claimed A was guilty? Again the Jabberwocky could not have known (both 2A and 2B would be possible). Now Case 3 is a different story: The only possibility under this case in which there is at least one lie and at least one truth is 3C;

so if the Jabberwocky were told that A claimed to be innocent, B claimed to be guilty, and C claimed A to be innocent, he would have known that C was guilty. So it is possible the Jabberwocky *was* told this. Now, if the reader will examine the remaining cases—Cases 4, 5, 6, 7, 8—he will see that Case 6 is the only one (other than Case 3) where the Jabberwocky could tell who was guilty, and (like Case 3) it turns out to be C. So either the Jabberwocky was told the statements of Case 3 or the statements of Case 6, and in both cases it turns out (by a fortunate coincidence!) that C was guilty.

### ♛ 84

ANOTHER CASE   We know that A accused B, and we don't know what B or C said. Suppose we were given the additional information that the guilty one is the only one who lied. Then any of the three could be guilty; there is no way to tell which one. On the other hand, if we were told that the guilty one was the only one who told the truth, then we would know that A couldn't be guilty (for if he were, he would have told the truth when he accused B, which would mean that B was guilty) and that B couldn't be guilty (for if he were, then A would have been innocent and also would have told the truth about B); so it would have to be C who was guilty. Therefore, the Red Queen must have been told that the guilty one was the only one who told the truth; otherwise she could never have known who was guilty. So the answer is that C is guilty.

### ♛ 85

AND THIS CASE? Suppose Humpty Dumpty had been told that all three lied. Then he couldn't have known whether C was guilty and accused A, or whether A was guilty and C accused himself (since all three would have lied in either case).

It is impossible that Humpty Dumpty was told that all three told the truth, because it couldn't be that all three told the truth (since A, B both accused B, and C accused someone other than B).

If Humpty Dumpty had been told that there were exactly two lies, then he would have known that it was A and B who lied (because if either told the truth, so did the other who agreed with him) and that C told the truth. Then either C accused himself and was guilty, or he accused A and A was guilty, but there is no way to tell which. So Humpty Dumpty couldn't have known who was guilty in this case.

The only possibility that Humpty Dumpty could have known who was guilty is that he was told that exactly two statements were true. This means that A, B both told the truth (because their statements agreed, so if one were false, the other would also be false, which would mean two false statements) and C lied. Since A, B both told the truth and accused B, then B must be guilty.

### ♛86

WHAT WAS THE FATE OF THE GOAT   Given the fact that the Goat lied, it does not follow that the Goat was guilty, nor does it follow that the Goat was innocent; so, knowing that the Court knew that the Goat lied, the Court might have convicted the Goat (on the basis of further evidence, which we don't know about), or they might have acquitted him (again, on the basis of further evidence), or they might have done neither, and there is no way of knowing which. On the other hand, if both Insects told the truth, it must follow that the Goat was guilty, because both Insects accused the same creature (since they both told the truth) and neither accused himself; so they must have both accused the Goat. So the Gentleman in white paper must have been told that both Insects told the truth, in order for him to have known what the Court did. He then knew that the Court convicted the Goat.

### ♛87

THE MOST BAFFLING CASE OF ALL   To solve this remarkable puzzle, we must use the table used in the solution of Problem 83.

To begin with, the Jabberwocky solved the case after knowing which of the eight cases occurred (that is, knowing what each defendant said) and knowing that at most one defendant told the truth. This rules out Cases 4, 6, 7, 8, because in Case 4, there are two possibilities (4A and 4C) in which at most one defendant told the truth; in Case 6 there are again two possibilities (6B and 6C); in Case 7 there are the two possibilities 7A and 7C; and in Case 8 there are the two possibilities 8B and 8C. So, in none of these four cases could the Jabberwocky have known who was guilty. On the other hand, in Case 1, possibility 1A is the only one in which there was at most one true statement; in Case 2, 2B is the only possibility; in Case 3, 3A is the only one; and in Case 5, 5B is the only one. So we know that one of the Cases 1, 2, 3, 5 is the one which actually holds.

Now, Tweedledee was told that the Jabberwocky solved the problem, so Tweedledee also knew that the actual case was either 1, 2, 3, or 5. If he had been told that A claimed to be guilty, then he would have ruled out Cases 1, 2, and 3 and known that Case 5 must hold, which means that B is guilty (because 5B is the only possibility under Case 5 in which at most one true statement was made). This means that Tweedledee would have solved the problem, but we are given that Tweedledee *didn't* solve the problem; therefore, he was not told that A claimed to be guilty; he was told that A claimed to be innocent, so he knew that Case 5 didn't hold, but he had no way of knowing whether Case 1, 2, or 3 held; hence he didn't know whether A or B was guilty. Anyway, we now know that one of the Cases 1, 2, or 3 holds.

Now we consider Tweedledum. He was told about the Jabberwocky, so he also knew that one of the Cases 1, 2, 3, 5 must hold, but he was not told about Tweedledee; so he did not know that Case 5 was ruled out. Now, he asked either about B or C, but we don't know which. Suppose he asked about B. If the White Knight told him that B claimed to be guilty, then Tweedledum would have ruled out Cases 1, 2, and 5, and would have been left just with Case 3; so he would have solved the problem (concluding that A was guilty). But he didn't solve the problem; so if he asked what B said, then he was told that B claimed to be innocent. So we now know that *if* Tweedledum asked what B said, then Case 1 or Case 2 holds.

Suppose Tweedledum asked what C said. If he had been told that C said that A was guilty, he would have eliminated Cases 1, 3, 5 and solved the problem (concluding that B was guilty). But he didn't solve the problem, so he must have been told that C claimed that A was innocent. This means that Case 1 or Case 3 holds, and A must be guilty (though Tweedledum couldn't know this, because as far as he was concerned, Case 5 could also hold and B could be guilty).

We now see that if Tweedledum asked about B, then (since he didn't solve the problem) either Case 1 or Case 2 holds. If he asked about C, then either Case 1 or Case 3 holds. Now, Humpty Dumpty asked whether Tweedledum inquired about B or about C. If he had been told that Tweedledum inquired about B, then Humpty Dumpty would know that either Case 1 or Case 2 holds, and hence that either A or B was guilty, but he couldn't have told which. But Humpty Dumpty was able to solve the problem; therefore, he must have been told that Tweedledum inquired about C; so Humpty Dumpty then knew that either Case 1 or Case 3 held, and that A is the guilty one in each case. This proves that A was guilty.

## Chapter 11

🐦 88

A QUESTION Yes, they do follow. Let us first consider Proposition 1: Suppose a person believes he is awake. Either he really is awake or he isn't. Suppose he is awake. Then his belief is correct, but anyone who has a correct belief while awake must be of Type A. Suppose, on the other hand, that he is asleep. Then his belief is incorrect, but anyone who has an incorrect belief while asleep must be of Type A. Therefore, whether he is awake or asleep, he must be of Type A. This proves Proposition 1.

As for Proposition 2, suppose a person believes he is of Type A. If he really is of Type A, then his belief is correct, but a person of Type A can have a correct belief only while he is awake. On the other hand, if he is of Type B, then his belief is incorrect, but a person of Type B can have an incorrect belief only while he is awake. So in either case he is awake, which proves Proposition 2.